For all portable keyboards *by Kenneth Baker.*

THE COMPLETE KEYBOARD PLAYER

OMNIBUS EDITION

BOOK 1

Two important features of Book One are
the pull-out chord chart, and the record,
on which the author plays selected songs and
exercises from Book One.

Exclusive Distributor:
Music Sales Corporation
225 Park Avenue South, New York, NY 10003 U.S.A.

Order No. AM 60476
International Standard Book Number: 0.8256.1063.X

Printed in the United States of America by
Vicks Lithograph and Printing Corporation

Amsco Publications
New York/London/Sydney/Cologne

ABOUT THIS BOOK

Welcome to the fascinating world of home music-making.

This course has been written to help you get the best out of your electronic keyboard — the most advanced and versatile musical instrument yet invented.

By the end of Book One you will be:

- Reading music.

- Playing popular melodies in many different styles.

- Adding complete accompaniments, consisting of bass notes, chords, and drums, to your songs.

- Creating a wealth of fascinating sounds.

Although written primarily as a "teach yourself" method, this course will be of great use to teachers, both private and classroom.

If you are teaching yourself to play, two important and helpful features of Book One are the pull-out chord chart, which fits over your keys, and the record, on which you can hear the author playing selected songs and exercises from the book.

LAYOUT OF THE KEYBOARD

1 Your electronic keyboard looks
something like this:—

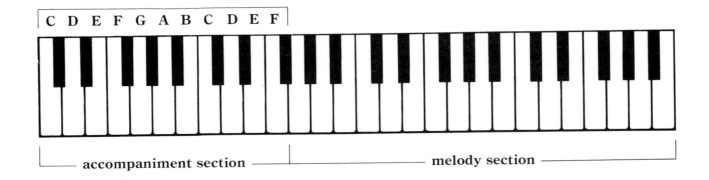

C D E F G A B C D E F

accompaniment section — melody section

The left hand section of the keyboard is
used for the **accompaniment.** Just
playing single notes here can give you a
truly professional-sounding background to
your songs.

The remainder of the keyboard is used
for the **melody.**

BLACK KEYS

2 The black keys are grouped like this:—

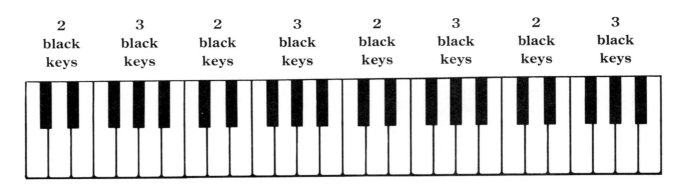

| 2 black keys | 3 black keys | 2 black keys | 3 black keys | 2 black keys | 3 black keys | 2 black keys | 3 black keys |

You need these black key groups in order
to locate the white keys.

NAMES OF THE NOTES

Punch out the cardboard "keyboard guide" which comes with this book. Select the one that fits, or most nearly fits your keyboard, and place it behind the keys.

You will see from the guide that there are only seven different letter names:

A   B   C   D   E   F   G

These keep repeating throughout the keyboard.

NOTE C

4

Let's learn "C" first.

Pick out all the C's from the guide (there will be three, four or five of them, depending on your keyboard model). Note that these C's lie directly to the left of each of the groups of two black keys:—

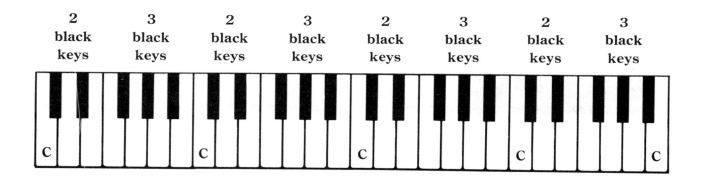

Remove your guide from the keys for a moment and locate all the C's without its help.

THE OTHER SIX NOTES

Use the black note groupings to locate **D, E, F, G, A,** and finally **B.** Check with your keyboard guide to begin with, then try locating the notes without the guide.

Spend a little time each day "note finding", and before you know it, you will be able to dispense with your keyboard guide altogether — which means, of course, that you can concentrate more on the **music.**

SINGLE-FINGER CHORDS

6 Now let's start to play.

Switch on your keyboard and select "single-finger chords" (refer to your owner's manual for the position of this function).

In the "accompaniment" section of your keyboard, play the note C with the index finger of your left hand. If you have a choice of two C's, play the upper one, i.e. the one to the right:—

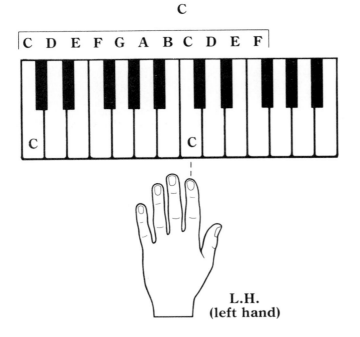

L.H.
(left hand)

You are hearing a chord of "C" (three notes playing together).

FINGERED CHORDS

7 This is an alternative, and far more productive way of using your left hand. I advise you to adopt it right from the start.

Switch on your keyboard and select "fingered chords" (refer to your owner's manual).

In the "accompaniment" section of your keyboard, play the following three notes together:—

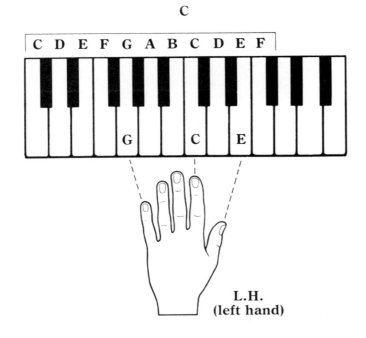

L.H.
(left hand)

This time you are hearing, and actually playing, a chord of C.

RHYTHM

8

Now let's add rhythm to your chord of C.

In the section of your instrument marked "rhythm", select "Rock". Press the start button and a rock-style drum rhythm will begin. Set the "tempo" (speed) button control to "medium".

Play and hold the note C (if using the "single-finger chord" method), or play and hold the complete C chord (if using the "fingered chord" method). You will hear an accompaniment, consisting of:—

bass note(s)

chord of C

drums

MEMORY

9

If you have a "memory" button press it now. This will "lock" the C chord into the memory, and you may remove your left hand from the keyboard altogether.

Try other rhythm patterns, such as "Swing", "Waltz", "Bossa Nova", and so on. Leave the memory button on, and the keyboard will continue to play on its own.

When you have finished experimenting with the rhythms come back to "Rock", and stop the rhythm.

FINGER NUMBERS

10

Your fingers are numbered from 1 to 5, like this:—

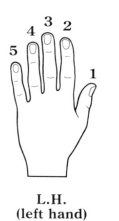

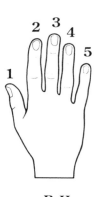

L.H.
(left hand)

R.H.
(right hand)

- Your left hand plays the accompaniment.

- Your right hand plays the melody.

G CHORD

11 In order to play the accompaniment to your first song, *Merrily We Roll Along,* you need to learn a new chord: G.

Using single-finger chord method:

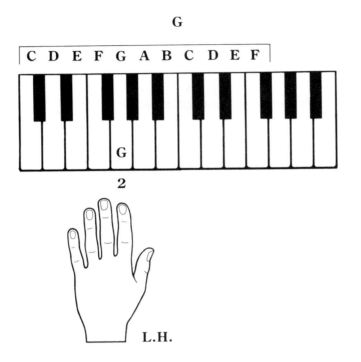

Using fingered chord method:

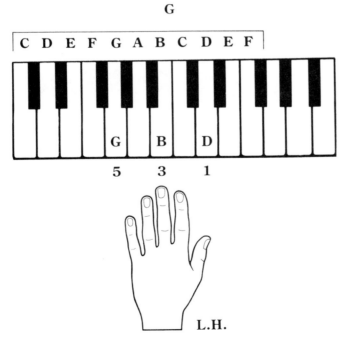

Before going any further, check your keyboard settings:—

Single-finger chords, or fingered chords + Memory (if available).

Rhythm: rock

Tempo: medium

PLAYING C AND G CHORDS, WITH RHYTHM

12 Press the rhythm "start" button with your right hand exactly as your left hand plays the "C" Chord. The accompaniment will begin.

Alternatively, press the "synchro-start" button (if you have one). The accompaniment will begin as soon as your left hand strikes the first note(s).

Let the C Chord and its rhythm play for a while, then change to the G Chord.

After a while change back to C.

NOTES ON CHORD CHANGING

13 When using the single-finger chord method:

- Play only one note at a time. Never let notes overlap.

When using the fingered chord method, without "memory":

- If the chords being changed have a note in common, don't bother to re-strike that note. e.g.:

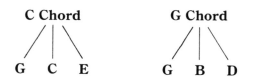

- The note G is common to both chords, so hold it down throughout any chord changing.

When using either chord method:

- If you have a flashing "tempo" light*, try to change your chords on a flash (more of this later).

* refer to your owner's manual.

USING THE RECORD

14

Now listen to band 1 (the accompaniment to "Merrily We Roll Along") of the record included with this book. The written music for this appears below. Follow the music through as you listen to the record.

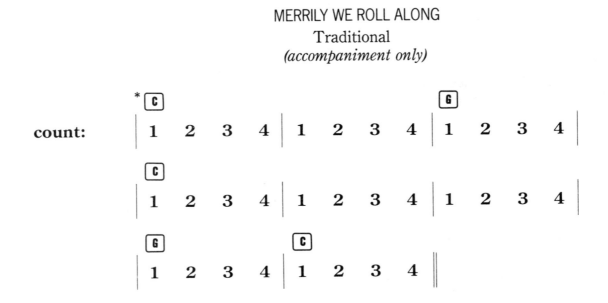

MERRILY WE ROLL ALONG
Traditional
(accompaniment only)

Notice how my counting on the record fits in naturally with the rhythm of the drums. Notice also that the counting tells you where to change chords.

Listen to the record again and play your chords along with it. Note: Don't press your "rhythm start" button this time. This is because it is virtually impossible to **synchronize** the rhythm sections of two keyboard instruments, so use only the rhythm section on the record.

Are you changing your chords cleanly and at the right time? . . .

Play the piece on your own now, using your own rhythm accompaniment.

* If you do not have a "memory" function on your keyboard, hold each chord down until the next chord symbol appears.

ACCENTS AND BAR LINES

15 While you were playing, did you feel a natural accent occurring on every count "1"?

$$\underline{1} \quad 2 \quad 3 \quad 4 \quad , \quad \underline{1} \quad 2 \quad 3 \quad 4 \quad \text{(etc.)}$$

If you have a tempo light, this is where it is designed to flash: on every count 1.

Play again and check this out.

If you look again at the music to *Merrily We Roll Along*, you will see that a series of vertical lines, called "bar lines", have been drawn in front of every count 1:—

MERRILY WE ROLL ALONG

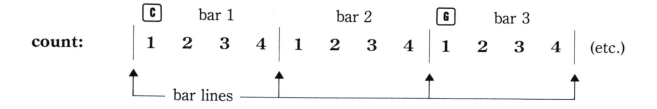

As well as indicating the position of the natural accents, bar lines divide the music up into "bars", or "measures". So every song has a bar 1, a bar 2, and so on.

WALTZ: BARCAROLLE

16

In "Merrily We Roll Along" there were 4 beats (counts) to the bar.

In your next song, *Barcarolle*, the natural accents occur every 3 beats (counts). Barcarolle can therefore be said to have "3 beats in a bar". Such a song is called a "Waltz".

Before you play *Barcarolle*, set your keyboard as follows:—

Single-finger chords, or fingered chords, + Memory (if available).

Rhythm: waltz

Tempo: medium.

Listen to the record first (band 2), to get the feel of the song, then play along with the following (chords only, no rhythm):—

BARCAROLLE

Offenbach

	C						G					
count:	1	2	3	1	2	3	1	2	3	1	2	3

						C						
	1	2	3	1	2	3	1	2	3	1	2	3

						G						
	1	2	3	1	2	3	1	2	3	1	2	3

						C						
	1	2	3	1	2	3	1	2	3	1	2	3

Did you follow the record?...

All right, press your rhythm "start" button now and play the piece on your own. Don't forget to count the beats.

PLAYING THE MELODY: MIDDLE C

17 Now let's learn how to play melodies, so that you can play the complete versions of *Merrily We Roll Along*, and *Barcarolle*.

Look again at your "keyboard guide" and you will see that one of the C's is circled. This C, which lies roughly in the middle of the instrument, is called Middle C:—

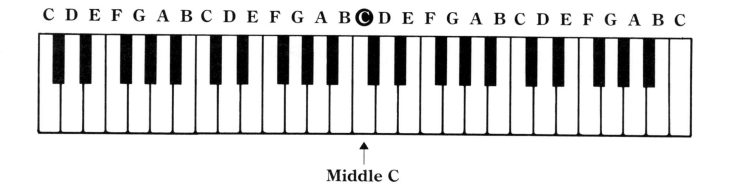

Middle C

Most of your first melody playing will take place around Middle C.

Place your right thumb (finger number 1)

on Middle C and cover the next four adjacent notes with the tips of your remaining four fingers:—

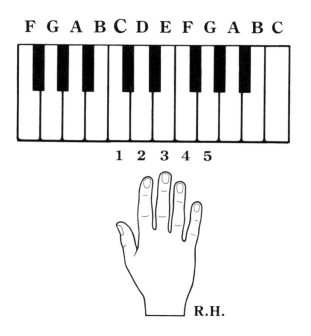

The notes covered in the above diagram are:

MIDDLE C, D, E, F, G

THE WRITTEN MUSIC

18 This is how these five notes are written down in music:—

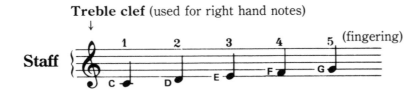

Notice how two of the notes (E, G) appear on lines, two of the notes (D, F) appear in spaces, and one of the notes (Middle C) has its own little line (called a "ledger" line).

TIMING

19 The staff (the group of five long lines, shown above) determines the "pitch" of the notes. It tells you whether the note is C, D, E, etc. But you need to know also how long each note is to last. This aspect of music, called "timing", is written like this:—

time note	name	lasting
♩ or 𝅗	quarter note (crotchet)	1 beat (or count)
♩ or 𝅗	half note (minim)	2 beats (or counts)
♩. or 𝅗	dotted half note (dotted minim)	3 beats (or counts)
o	whole note (semibreve)	4 beats (or counts)

Here are some examples of written notes, showing both "pitch" and "time":—

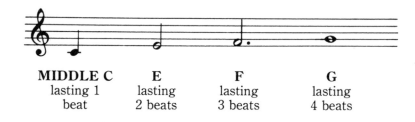

MIDDLE C	**E**	**F**	**G**
lasting 1 beat	lasting 2 beats	lasting 3 beats	lasting 4 beats

REGISTRATION

20 You are almost ready now to play the melody of "Merrily We Roll Along".

First you must set up the right hand (melody) section of your keyboard:—

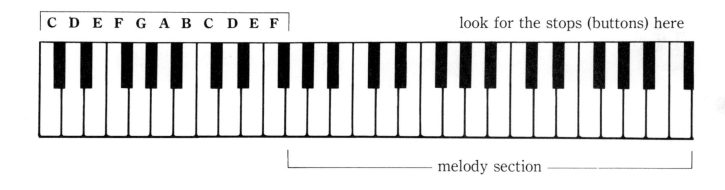

look for the stops (buttons) here

melody section

There are many different sounds available in your melody section*. There are orchestral sounds, such as flute, trumpet, and violin; percussive sounds such as piano, harpsichord, and vibes; and "odd" sounds such as synthe, fantasy, funny, and so on. Feel free to experiment with these different effects and don't be afraid to change your mind each time you play.

Sound set ups are called "registrations", and I will be giving "suggested registrations" for each piece, which you may, or may not, wish to follow.

★ refer to your owner's manual for details.

MERRILY WE ROLL ALONG

Traditional

Suggested registration: piano

Rhythm: rock
Tempo: medium (♩ = 88)*

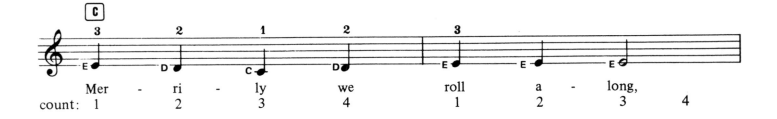

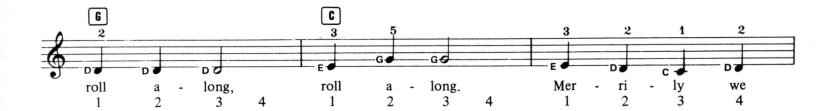

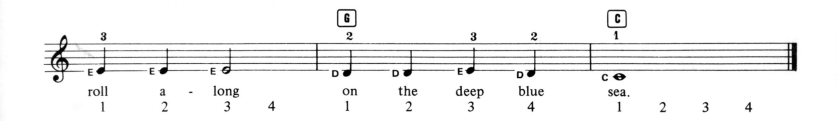

* Metronome marking. A metronome is an instrument which indicates the speed of a piece of music. Although not absolutely necessary, you may buy one if you wish at your local music dealer.

SUGGESTED PRACTICE ROUTINE FOR "MERRILY WE ROLL ALONG"

21

1. Listen to *Merrily We Roll Along* on the record (band 3), following the written music through as you do so.

2. Play the melody on its own with your right hand. You begin on note "E" with your 3rd finger.

3. When you are reasonably fluent with the notes, start to count the beats (1, 2, 3, 4, and so on). At this stage it may help if you add "drums" (no left hand chords). Start playing your melody WITH the tempo light; it flashes every four beats with this Rock rhythm.

4. Play your melody along with the record.

5. Revise the accompaniment. Play the accompaniment through (left hand only), counting 1, 2, 3, 4, etc. Check your accompaniment against the record if necessary.

6. Play accompaniment only and hum the melody through with it. This is an important stage. Try and imagine playing the melody notes as you do this.

7. Play melody and accompaniment together. Note: To help you get started, let the accompaniment run for a few bars on Chord C before coming in with the melody. Always start your melody on a tempo light.

8. If you wish, you may now play your complete *Merrily We Roll Along* with the record, **but do not press your "rhythm start" button.**

TIME SIGNATURE

22

Now let's play *Barcarolle*.

This song, you will remember, has three beats to the bar. These beats are quarter notes (crotchets):

This is indicated at the beginning of the piece, like this:— **3/4**

meaning: three 'quarter notes' to the bar.

This is called: the Time Signature.

SUGGESTED PRACTICE ROUTINE FOR "BARCAROLLE"

23

1. Listen to "Barcarolle" on the record (band 4), following it through with the written music.

2. Play the melody on its own. Count the timing (1, 2, 3, etc.)

3. Play the melody along with the record.

4. Revise the accompaniment.

5. Play the accompaniment and hum the melody through with it.

6. Play melody and accompaniment together.

TIES

24

Each of the time notes:—

		lasting
♩	quarter note (crotchet)	1 beat
♩	half note (minim)	2 beats
♩.	dotted half note (dotted minim)	3 beats
o	whole note (semibreve)	4 beats

may be extended by the use of a TIE. A tie is a curved line connecting two notes of the same pitch:—

Barcarolle (bars 7 and 8, and bars 15 and 16)

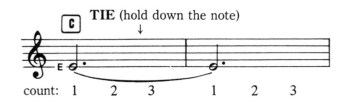

Here you play the first E and count for the second E also without striking the note again. Total time: 6 beats.

Look out for more ties in the songs which follow.

Work out your own "practice routine" for the new songs, using the record as before.

BARCAROLLE
(FROM "THE TALES OF HOFFMANN")

By Jacques Offenbach

Suggested registration: horn, or trumpet

Rhythm: Waltz
Tempo: medium (♩ = 88)

TIME SIGNATURE

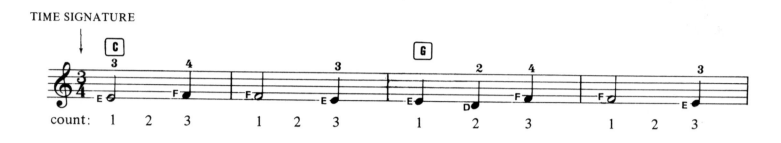

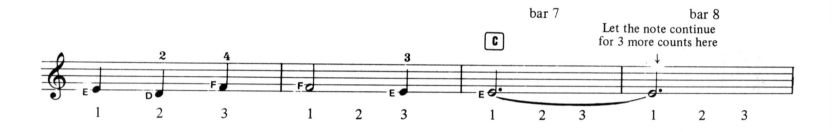

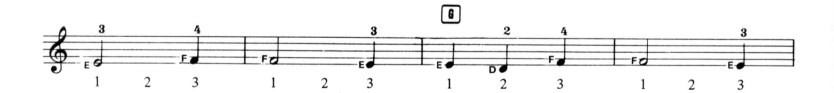

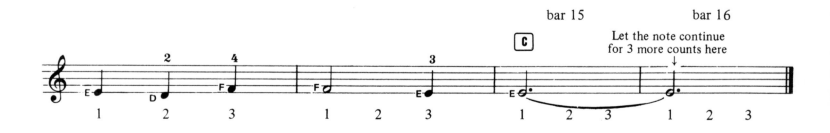

LIGHTLY ROW

Traditional

Suggested registration: trumpet

Rhythm: swing
Tempo: medium (♩ = 92)

TIME SIGNATURE:
4 quarter notes in a bar

WHITE ROSE OF ATHENS

Music by Manos Hadjidakis
Words by Norman Newell
Additional Words by Archie Bleyer

Suggested registration: clarinet
+ arpeggio (if available)

Rhythm: rhumba
Tempo: fairly slow (♩ = 84)

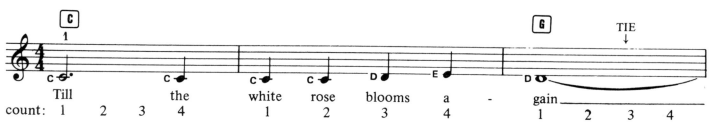

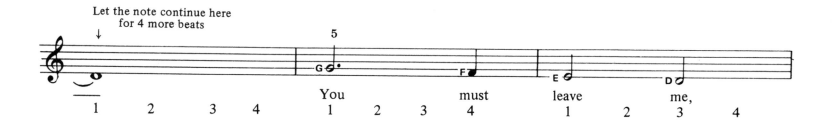

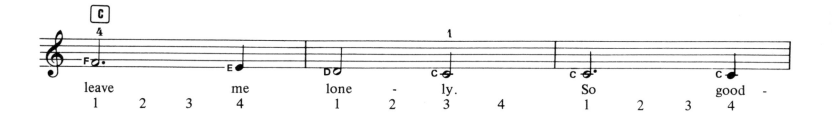

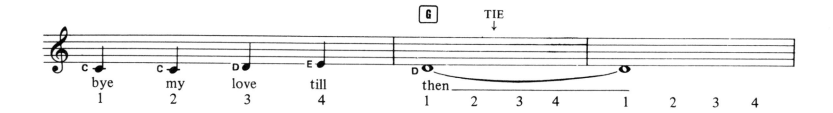

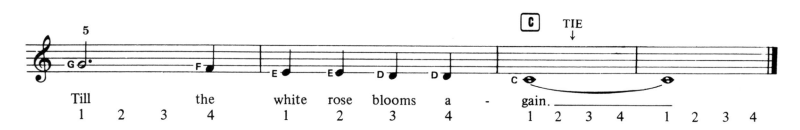

NEW CHORD: F

Using single-finger chord method:

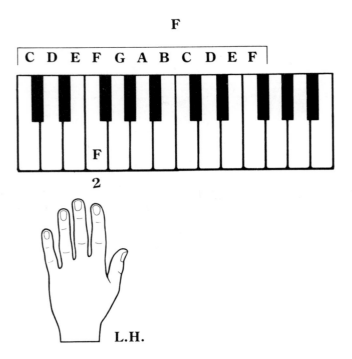

Using fingered chord method:

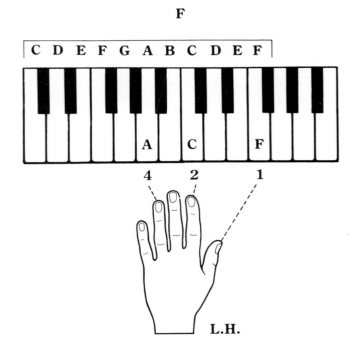

PICK-UP NOTES

26 Songs do not always begin on beat 1. In your next song: *Banks Of The Ohio,* the melody has three notes before the first beat 1. These preliminary notes are called "pick-up notes":—

BANKS OF THE OHIO, p. 24

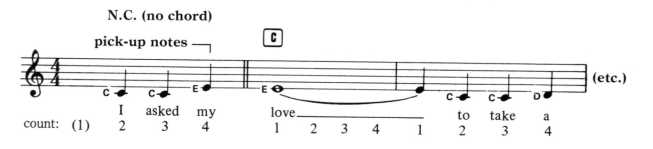

Beats missing from the pick-up bar appear (usually) in the last bar of the song:—

BANKS OF THE OHIO

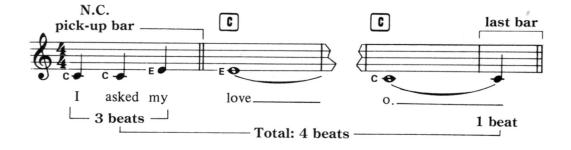

Note: It is usual to play "no chord", written: "N.C.", during pick-up notes.

BANKS OF THE OHIO

Traditional

Suggested registration: flute

Rhythm. rhumba, or beguine
Tempo: medium (♩ = 100)
Synchro-start, if available

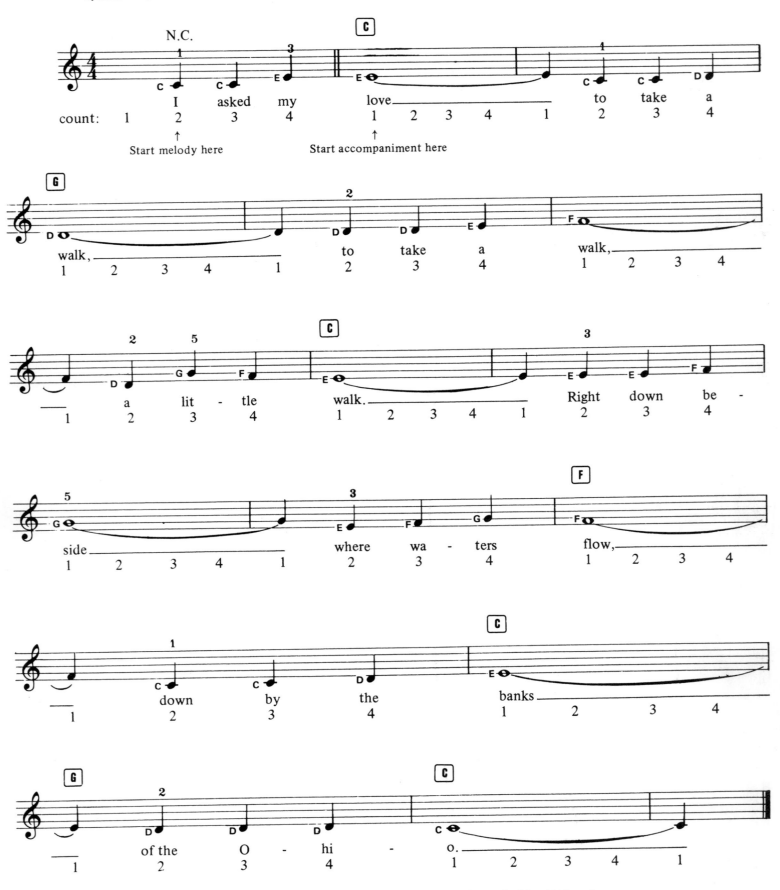

WHEN THE SAINTS GO MARCHING IN

Traditional

Suggested registration: trumpet

Rhythm: swing
Tempo: moderately fast (♩ = 138)
Synchro-start, if available

THREE NEW NOTES: A, B, C, FOR RIGHT HAND

FINGERING NEW NOTES

28 When any new notes appear extend your hand to play them. Allow your hand to return to its normal relaxed position (one finger per note) as soon as possible:—

LARGO, p. 28

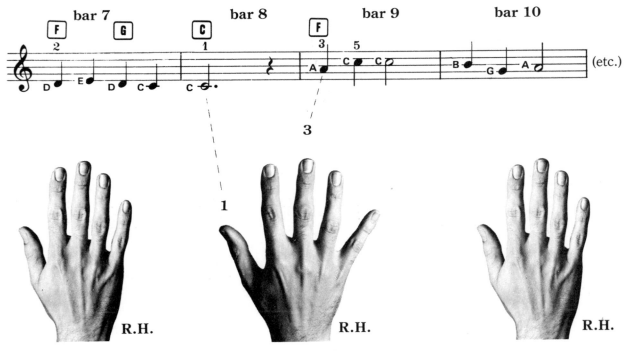

normal hand position (covering C, D, E, F, G)

extend hand

normal hand position (now covering F, G, A, B, C)

Follow the written fingering and you can't go wrong.

RESTS

29 Silences are often called for in music. In order to indicate these, symbols called "rests" are used. Each of the Time Notes has its own rest:—

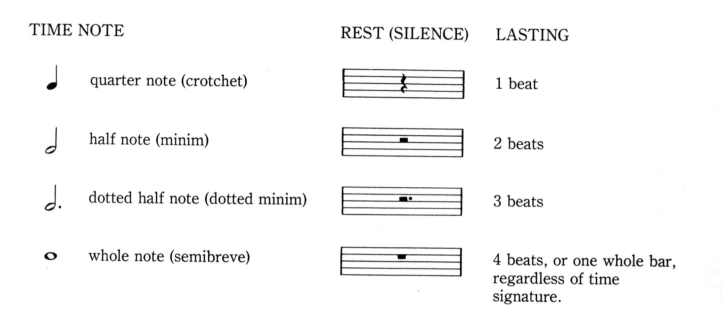

TIME NOTE		REST (SILENCE)	LASTING
♩	quarter note (crotchet)	𝄽	1 beat
♩	half note (minim)	▬	2 beats
♩.	dotted half note (dotted minim)	▬.	3 beats
𝅝	whole note (semibreve)	▬	4 beats, or one whole bar, regardless of time signature.

Rests are used mainly for musical or dramatic reasons. However, they are often useful for moving your hand from one part of the keyboard to another:—

LARGO, p. 28

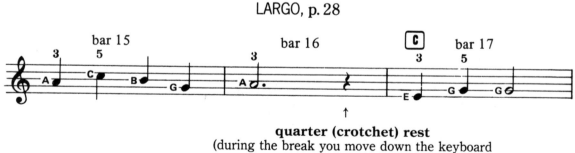

quarter (crotchet) rest
(during the break you move down the keyboard
to a new hand position)

LARGO
("FROM THE NEW WORLD")
By Antonin Dvořák

Suggested registration: oboe

Rhythm: bossa nova
Tempo: slow (♩ = 80)

MICHAEL ROW THE BOAT ASHORE

Traditional

Suggested registration: jazz organ
        + tremolo

Rhythm: rock
Tempo: medium ($\quad$ = 100)
Synchro-start, if available

Start melody here   Start accompaniment here

* Repeat Mark. Go back to the matching
sign ‖: and play through again until
"FINE": the end of the piece.

WOODEN HEART

Words & Music by Fred Wise, Ben Weisman, Kay
Twomey & Berthold Kaempfert

Suggested registration: *piano*

Rhythm: swing
Tempo: moderately fast (♩ = 144)
Synchro-start, if available

* Re-strike the note with a different
finger, as shown.

THIS OLE HOUSE

Words & Music by Stuart Hamblen

Suggested registration: saxophone

Rhythm: swing
Tempo: fast ($\quad$ = 208)
Synchro-start, if available

* The part of the song which contains the
bulk of the narrative. Usually sung by a
solo singer.

* The part of the song where everybody joins in.

EIGHTH NOTES (QUAVERS)

30 The eighth note, or quaver, is another sort of time note:—

eighth notes (quavers)

Eighth notes move twice as fast as your basic quarter note (crotchet) beat:—

So each eighth note is worth half a beat.

If you say the word "and" in between your beat numbers you will get the feel of the eighth note:—

eighth note example:

count: 1   2   3   4   1 and 2 and 3 and 4 and

Listen to this example on the record (band 10). Notice how I keep the speed of my basic beats the same throughout.

Like the other time notes, the eighth note has its own rest—

eighth (quaver) rest	equivalent to	lasting
		½ (quarter note) beat

Count eighth rests in exactly the same way that you would count eighth notes:—

SUPER TROUPER, p. 36

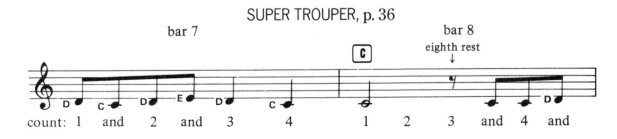

count: 1 and 2 and 3 4   1 2 3 and 4 and

LEGATO AND STACCATO

31 **Legato** means "connected." When you play legato, you move smoothly from finger to finger, leaving no gaps between notes.

Notes which are to be played legato are indicated on the music by a curved line, called a "slur", or "phrase mark":—

DANCE LITTLE BIRD, p.37

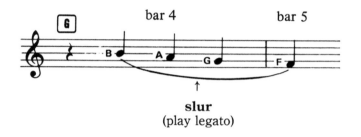

slur
(play legato)

When there are no slurs, or other markings to the contrary, assume that you are to play legato.

Staccato means "cut short". It is the opposite of "legato". Release the note as soon as you have played it, using a "pecking" movement of the hand.

Notes which are to be played staccato are indicated on the music by dots above, or below the note(s):—

DANCE LITTLE BIRD, p. 37

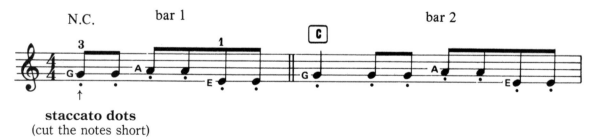

staccato dots
(cut the notes short)

SUPER TROUPER

Words & Music by Benny Andersson & Bjorn Ulvaeus

Suggested registration: guitar

Rhythm: rock
Tempo: medium (♩ = 116)

DANCE LITTLE BIRD

Words & Music by Werner Thomas & Terry Rendall

Suggested registration: banjo

Rhythm: cha-cha (or rock)
Tempo: medium (♩ = 120)
Synchro-start, if available

* re-strike the note with a different
finger, as shown.

32

ANNIE'S SONG

Words & Music by John Denver

Suggested registration: flute

Rhythm: waltz
Tempo: moderately fast (♩ = 132)
Synchro-start, if available

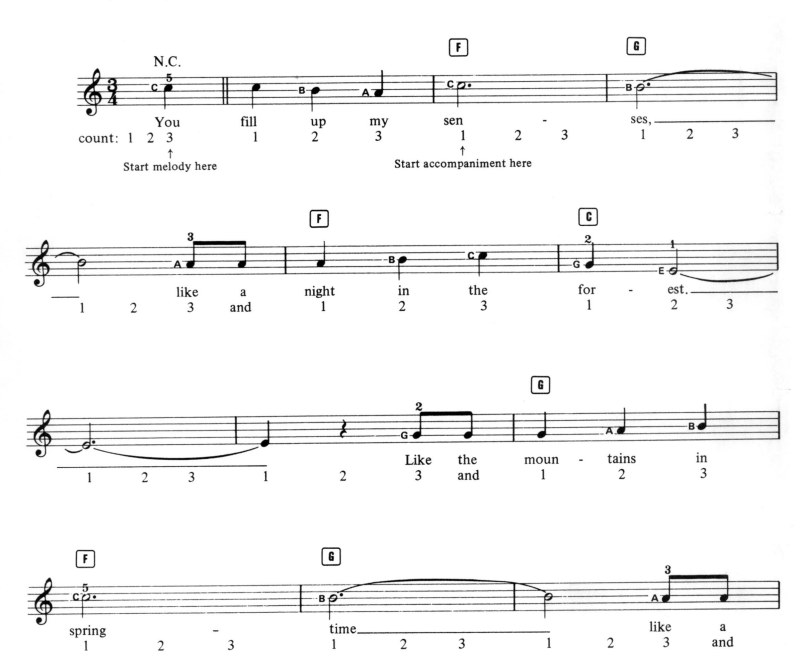

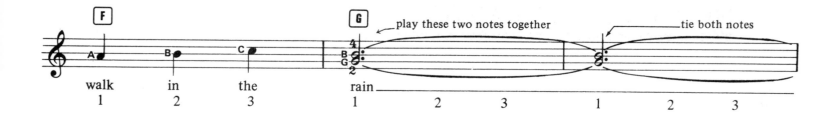

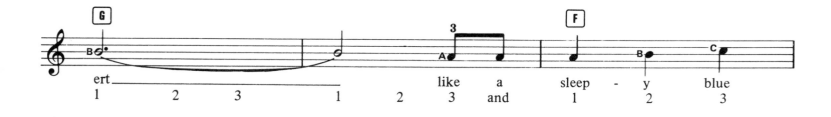

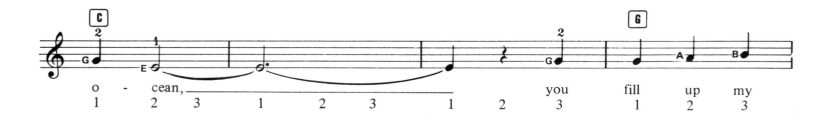

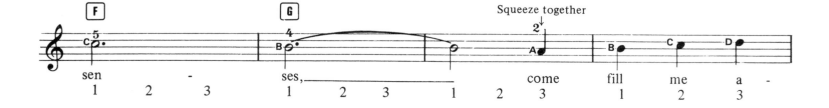

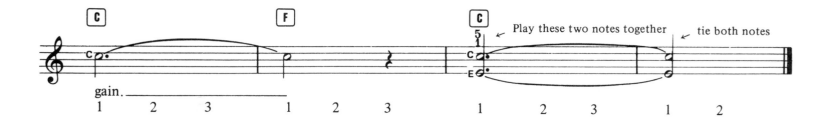

RIVERS OF BABYLON

Words & Music by Farian, Reyam, Dowe & McMaughton

Suggested registration: string ensemble + rock guitar

Rhythm: reggae (or rock)
Tempo: medium (♩ = 118)
Synchro-start, if available

Start melody here

Start accompaniment here

* Change rock guitar to synthe

* Section Lines. An old section is
over, and a new section is about to begin.

SEVENTH CHORDS

33

The three chords you have played so far: C, G, and F, are all "major" chords.

"Seventh" chords are variations of major chords.

When using the "single-finger chord" method, there are various ways of forming "sevenths". Your owner's manual will tell you exactly how to form 7ths on your particular instrument. However, the first two diagrams in 34, below, show two possibilities:

CHORD OF G7

34

Using single-finger chord method:

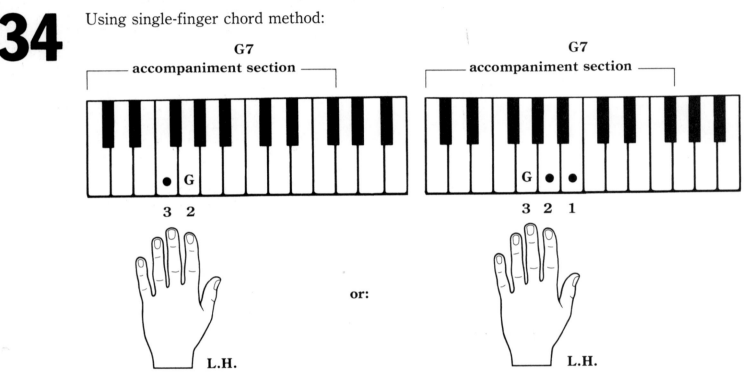

play G, together with any white note to its LEFT.

play G, together with any two notes to its RIGHT

Using fingered chord method:

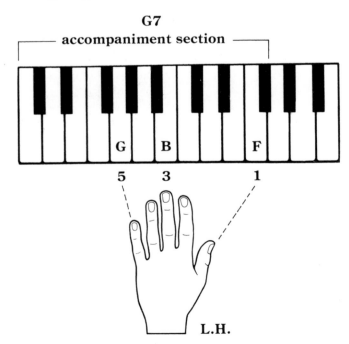

CHORD OF D7

35 Using single-finger chord method:

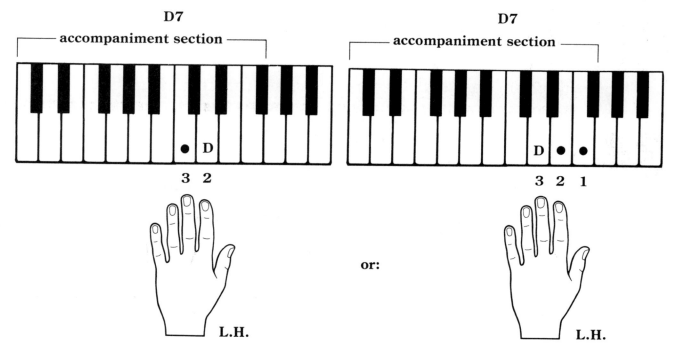

play D, together with any white note to its LEFT.

play D, together with any two notes to its RIGHT.

Using fingered chord method:

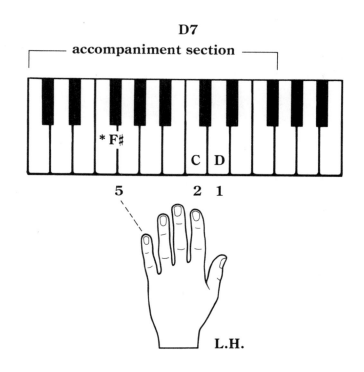

* Sharps and flats will be explained in Book Two. For now simply play the black note indicated.

EDELWEISS
(FROM "THE SOUND OF MUSIC")

Words by Oscar Hammerstein II
Music by Richard Rodgers

Suggested registration: string ensemble
(or violin solo). Arpeggio optional.
Rhythm: waltz
Tempo: fairly slow ($\,\downharpoonright$ = 80)

* If you are using the single-finger chord
method and have no 7th chords available
on your model, play "G",

DAL SEGNO AL FINE (D.S. AL FINE)

36

Dal Segno means "repeat from the 𝄋 sign". The sign looks like this: 𝄋

Fine is the end of the piece.

Dal Segno Al Fine (D.S. al Fine) means go back to the sign: 𝄋 , play through the same music as before until you reach the word "Fine", which is the end of the piece.

I'D LIKE TO TEACH THE WORLD TO SING

Words and Music by Roger Cook, Roger Greenaway, Billy Backer & Billy Davis

Suggested registration: vibraphone + sustain

Rhythm: swing
Tempo: medium (♩ = 120)
Synchro-start, if available

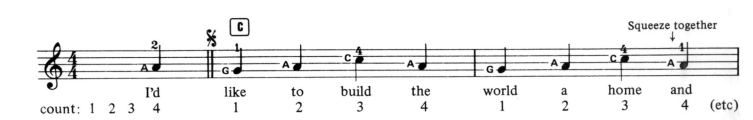

count: 1 2 3 4   1   2   3   4   1   2   3   4   (etc)

I'd like to build the world a home and

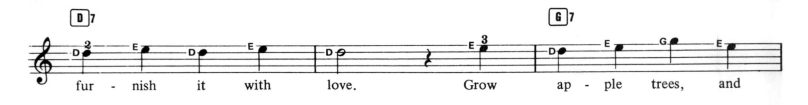

fur - nish it with love. Grow ap - ple trees, and

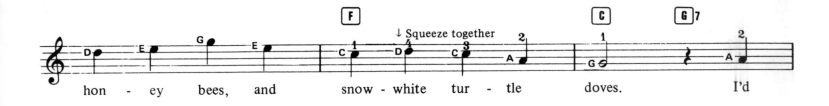

hon - ey bees, and snow - white tur - tle doves. I'd

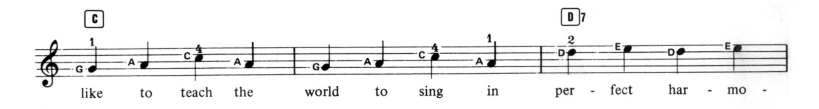

like to teach the world to sing in per - fect har - mo -

ny, I'd like to hold it in my arms and

* The SELECT, or SELECTOR button (in the melody section of your instrument), will change the sound from "vibraphone" to some other voice (depending on your model). Pressing the selector button is one of the easiest ways of making a registration change.

LAST WORD

37
So we come to the end of Book One of The Complete Keyboard Player. I am sure you are delighted with your progress so far.

In Book Two you will—

- learn about sharps and flats.
- increase the range of your melody playing.
- learn new chords, including minor chords.
- experiment with new sounds and rhythms.

Till then your last piece in this book is:

LET IT BE

Words & Music by John Lennon & Paul McCartney

Suggested registration: piano, or electric guitar

Rhythm: rock
Tempo: slow (♩ = 66)
Synchro-start, if available

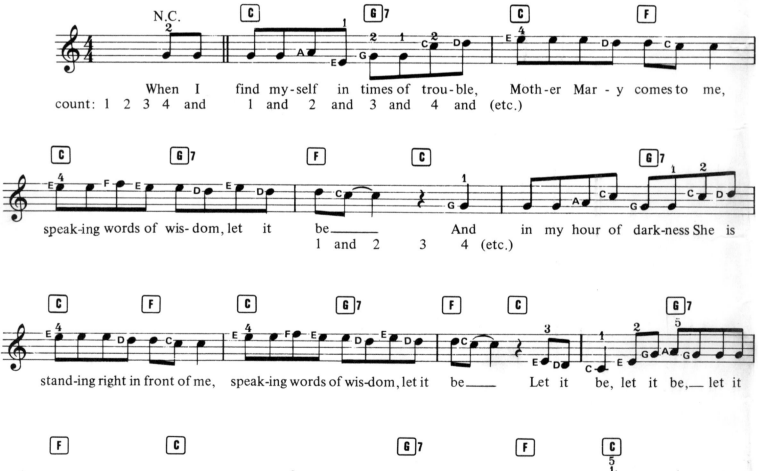

For all portable keyboards *by Kenneth Baker.*

THE COMPLETE KEYBOARD PLAYER

OMNIBUS EDITION

BOOK 2

Amsco Publications
New York/London/Sydney/Cologne

About This Book, 3

ABOUT THIS BOOK

In Book Two of The Complete Keyboard Player you take a giant step forward in reading musical notation.

Side by side with the single-finger chords, you continue your study of "fingered" chords, by far the most rewarding aspect of left hand accompaniment playing.

As the book progresses you play more and more fill-ins, double notes, and chords with your right hand, which helps give you that "professional" sound.

Although Book Two (like Book One of the series) is designed basically as a "teach yourself" method, teachers everywhere will find it ideal for training tomorrow's electronic keyboard players.

SHARPS, FLATS, AND NATURALS

1

This sign is a sharp: ♯

When you see a sharp written alongside a note, play the nearest available key (black or white) to the RIGHT of that note:—

written:

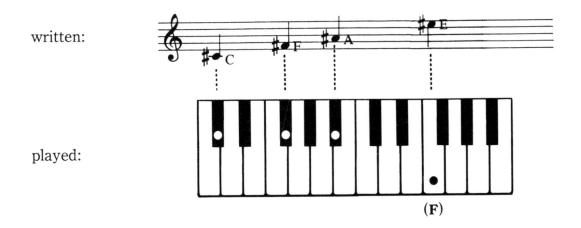

played:

(F)

Note: E sharp is simply an alternative way of writing "F".

This sign is a flat: ♭

When you see a flat written alongside a note, play the nearest available key (black or white) to the LEFT of that note:—

written:

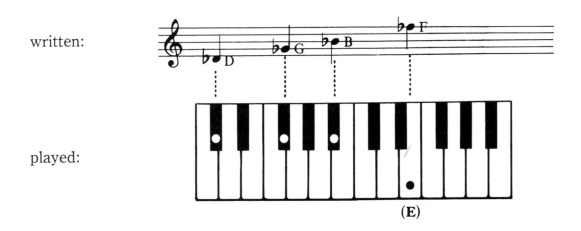

played:

(E)

Note: F flat is simply an alternative way of writing "E".

When a sharp or flat is written it
continues as a sharp or flat right through
the bar:—

At the next bar, however, everything
returns to normal:—

Apart from at the new bar, a sharp or flat
may be cancelled any time by a sign
called a "natural", ♮ :—

Look out for sharps, flats, and naturals in
the pieces which follow.

GET BACK

Words & Music by John Lennon & Paul McCartney

Suggested registration: electric guitar

Rhythm: rock
Tempo: medium (♩ = 120)

* **Common Time.** An alternative way of writing 𝄴

back to where you once be - longed___ Sweet Lo - ret - ta Mod - ern

thought she was a wo - man, but she was an - oth - er man,

All the girls a - round her say she's got it com - ing, but she gets it while she

can. Get back! Get back! Get

back to where you once be - longed___ Get back! Get back!

Get back to where you once be - longed. ___

* **Pause (Fermata).** Hold the note(s) longer
than written (at the discretion of the performer).

PIGALLE

English Lyrics by Charles Newman
French Lyrics by Georges Ulmer & Geo Koger
Music by Georges Ulmer & Guy Luypaerts

Suggested registration: accordion +
        chorus (chorale)

Rhythm: waltz
Tempo: fairly fast (♩ = 152)

ROCK AROUND THE CLOCK

Words & Music by Max C. Freedman & Jimmy de Knight

Suggested registration: trumpet, or saxophone

Rhythm: swing
Tempo: fairly fast (♩ = 160)

Press rhythm start button (ordinary, not synchro) with left hand, as right hand strikes first note. Play through Verse using melody and drums only. Start left hand chords at Chorus.

broad day - light, we're gon - na   rock,   gon - na rock   a -   round   the   clock   to -

night._____   When   the   clock   strikes   two,

three   and   four,   if   the   band   slows down   we'll   yell   for   more,   we're gon - na

rock   a - round   the   clock   to - night, we're gon - na   rock,   rock,   rock   till

broad day - light, we're gon - na   rock,   gon - na rock   a -   round   the   clock   to -

Add arpeggio

ff (very loud)

night.

getting louder
(increase your volume pedal,
if you have one.)

* ACCENT

TWO NEW CHORDS: C7 AND A7

2

Using single-finger chord method:

Locate "C" and "A" in the accompaniment section of your keyboard. Convert these notes into "C7" and "A7" (see Book One, p. 42ff., and your owner's manual).

Using fingered chord method:

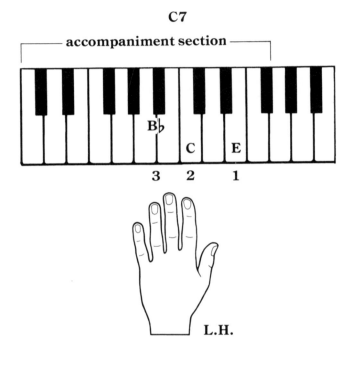

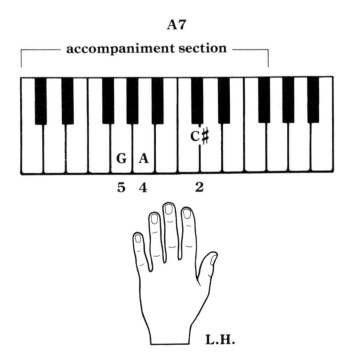

A NEW STAGE IN READING MUSIC

3 Up to now, in order to help you, letter names have appeared beside the written notes. These letters will now be discontinued.

Here's how you can learn the names of the notes:

The **staff** consists of five lines:—

remember this sentence:
Every **G**ood **B**oy **D**eserves **F**ruit

and four spaces:—

remember this word: **F A C E**

Learn the notes on the five lines, and the notes in the four spaces first. Then learn the "in-between" notes, like this:

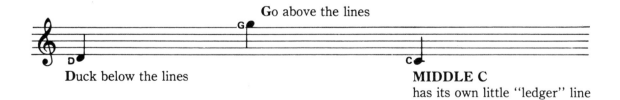

Go above the lines

Duck below the lines

MIDDLE C
has its own little "ledger" line

LET HIM GO, LET HIM TARRY

Traditional

Suggested registration: flute

Rhythm: bossa nova
Tempo: medium (♩ = 108)
Synchro-start, if available

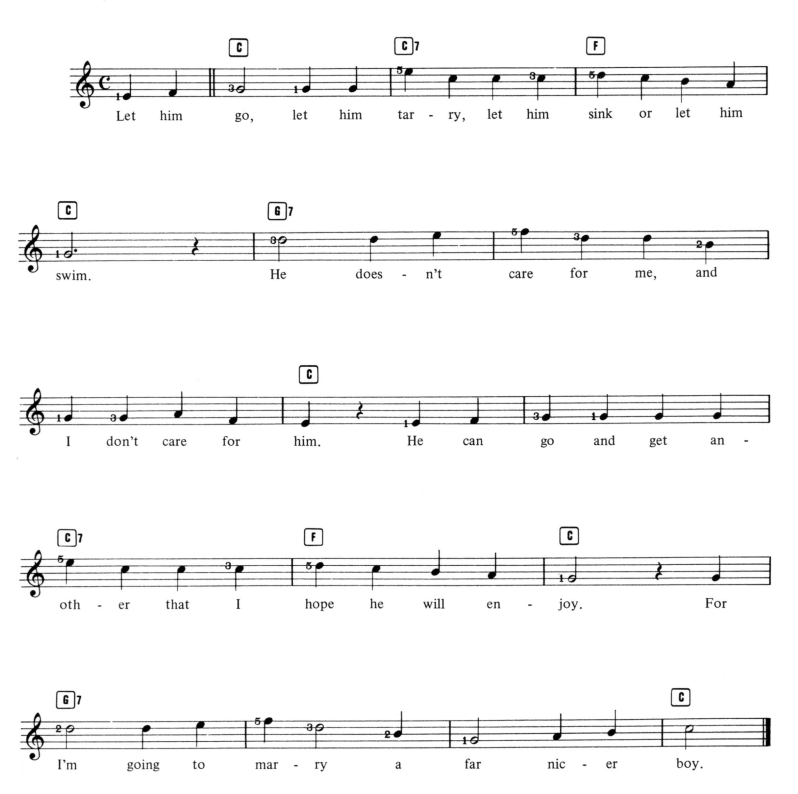

Let him go, let him tar - ry, let him sink or let him
swim. He does - n't care for me, and
I don't care for him. He can go and get an -
oth - er that I hope he will en - joy. For
I'm going to mar - ry a far nic - er boy.

LOVE ME TENDER

Words & Music by Elvis Presley & Vera Matson

Suggested registration: string ensemble.
Arpeggio optional.

Rhythm: rock
Tempo: medium (♩ = 96)

Love me ten - der, love me sweet, nev - er let me

go. You have made my life com - plete,

and I love you so. Love me ten - der,

love me true, all my dreams ful - fil.

For, my dar - lin', I love you, and I al - ways will.

DAL SEGNO AL CODA (D.S. AL CODA)

4 A **Coda** is a section, usually quite short, added to a piece of music to make an ending.

Dal Segno al Coda (D.S. al Coda) means go back to the sign: 𝄋 and play through the same music again, until:

to coda ⊕

From here jump to CODA and play through to the end.

SOMETHIN' STUPID
Words & Music by C. Carson Parks

Suggested registration: accordion

Rhythm: cha-cha (or rhumba)
Tempo: medium (♩ = 112)
Synchro-start, if available

I know I stand in line un-til you think you have the time to spend an eve -nin' with me____

____ And if we go some place to dance I know that there's a chance you won't be

leav - in' with me._____ Then af - ter - wards we drop in - to a

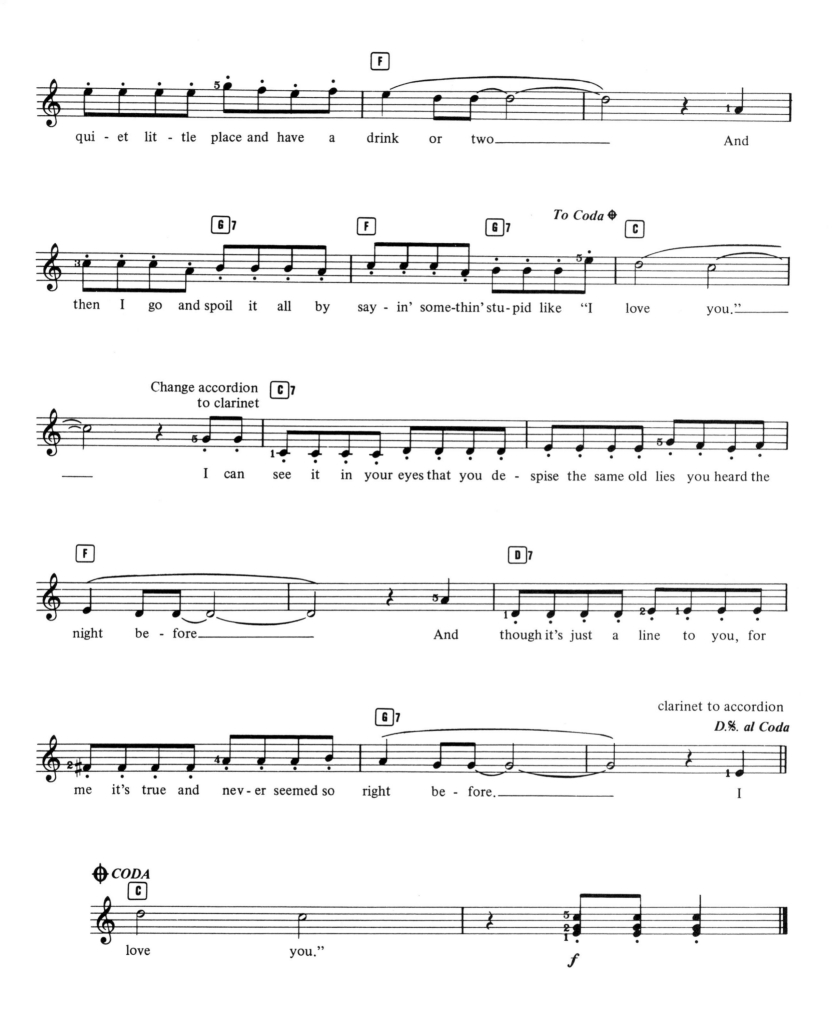

qui - et lit - tle place and have a drink or two_____ And

then I go and spoil it all by say - in' some-thin' stu - pid like "I love you."_____

Change accordion to clarinet

_____ I can see it in your eyes that you de - spise the same old lies you heard the

night be - fore_____ And though it's just a line to you, for

me it's true and nev - er seemed so right be - fore._____ I

clarinet to accordion
D.%. al Coda

⊕ *CODA*

love you."

f

ARE YOU LONESOME TONIGHT

Words & Music by Roy Turk & Lou Handman

Suggested registration: flute + full sustain

Rhythm: waltz
Tempo: fairly slow (♩ = 80)
Synchro-start, if available

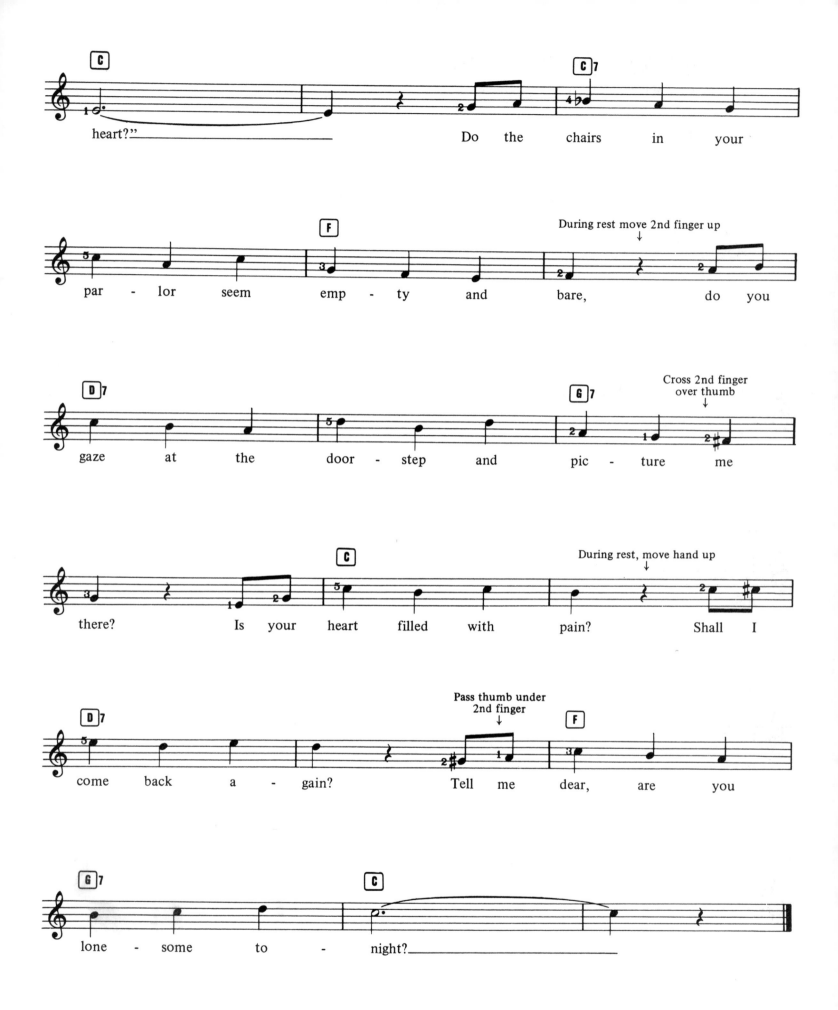

heart?"   Do the chairs in your

par - lor seem emp - ty and bare, do you

gaze at the door - step and pic - ture me

there?   Is your heart filled with pain? Shall I

come back a - gain? Tell me dear, are you

lone - some to - night?

AN APPLE FOR THE TEACHER

Words by Johnny Burke
Music by James V. Monaco

Suggested registration: trombone, or horn

Rhythm: swing
Tempo: fairly fast (♩ = 176)
Synchro-start, if available

THREE NEW NOTES FOR RIGHT HAND:
LOW G, A, B

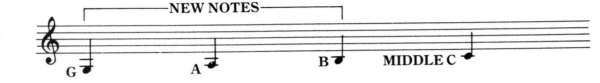

These three notes lie directly to the left of Middle C. The lowest of them, G, probably forms the left hand extremity of the "melody section" on your instrument.

I have placed letter names beside the new notes only in the next few songs.

GUANTANAMERA

Words by Jose Marti
Music adaptation by Hector Angulo & Pete Seeger

Suggested registration: flute, + duet (if available)

Rhythm: bossa nova
Tempo: medium (♩ = 100)

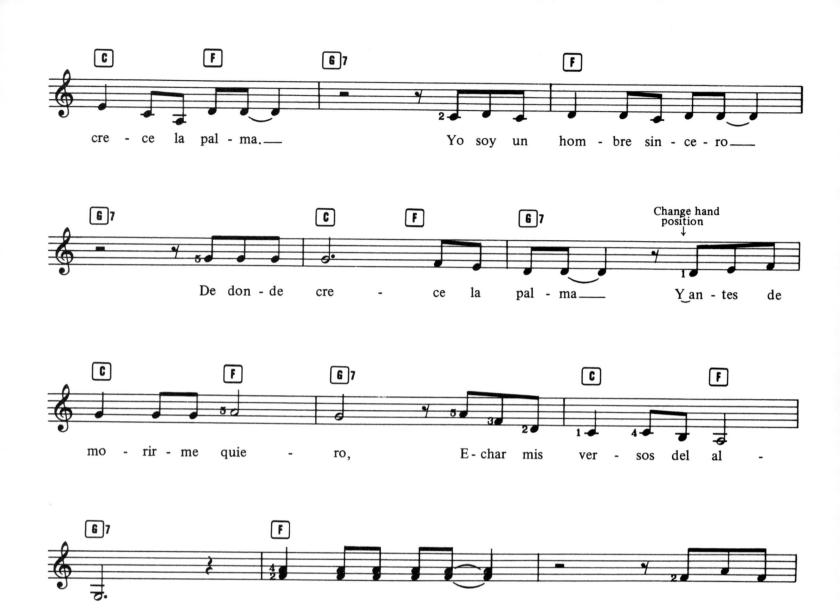

cre - ce la pal - ma.___ Yo soy un hom - bre sin - ce - ro___

De don - de cre - ce la pal - ma___ Y an - tes de

Change hand
position

mo - rir - me quie - ro, E - char mis ver - sos del al -

ma. Guan - ta - na - me - ra___ gua - ji - ra

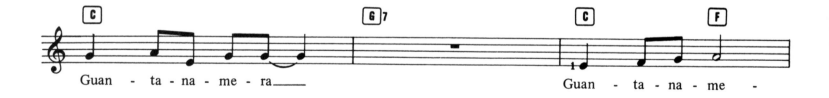

Guan - ta - na - me - ra___ Guan - ta - na - me -

ra, gua - ji - ra Guan - ta - na - me - ra!

BILL BAILEY WON'T YOU PLEASE COME HOME

Traditional

Suggested registration: *piano, or honky-tonk*
piano

Rhythm: *swing*
Tempo: *fairly fast* (♩ = 176)

DA CAPO AL CODA (D.C. AL CODA)

6

Da Capo means "from the beginning".

Da Capo al Coda (D.C. al Coda) means go back to the beginning of the piece and play through the same music again, until: to coda ⊕

From here jump to CODA and play through to the end.

THIS NEARLY WAS MINE

Words by Oscar Hammerstein II
Music by Richard Rodgers

Suggested registration: string ensemble

Rhythm: waltz
Tempo: slow (♩ = 80)

MINOR CHORDS

7 The MINOR CHORD is another important type of chord.

When using the single-finger chord function, there are various ways of forming minor chords. Your owner's manual will tell you how to form minor chords on your particular instrument. The first two diagrams in 8, on the next page, show two possibilities.

CHORD OF F MINOR (Fm)

Using single-finger chord method:

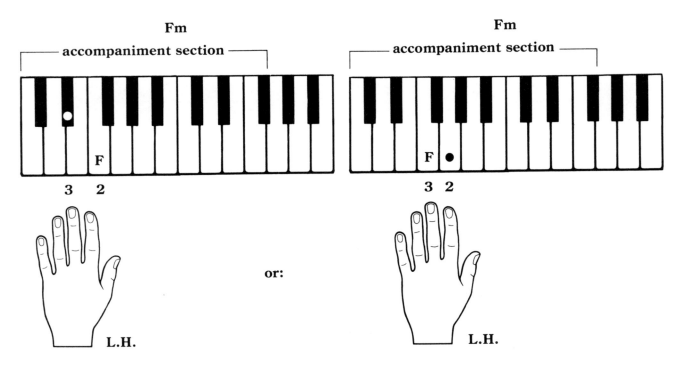

or:

play F, together with any black note to its LEFT.

play F, together with any (one) note to its RIGHT.

Using fingered chord method:

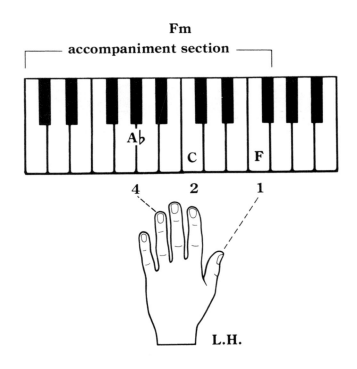

DOTTED TIME NOTES

9 A dot after a note adds half as much time again to that note:—

		lasting
♩	half note (minim)	2 beats
♩.	dotted half note (dotted minim)	2 + 1 = 3 beats
♩	quarter note (crotchet)	1 beat
♩.	dotted quarter note (dotted crotchet)	1 + ½ = 1½ beats

DOTTED QUARTER NOTE (DOTTED CROTCHET)

10 A Dotted Quarter Note, ♩., worth 1½ beats, usually combines with an Eighth Note (Quaver), ♪, worth ½ beat, to make two whole beats:—

♩. ♪   1½ + ½ = 2 beats

or: ♪ ♩.   ½ + 1½ = 2 beats

The first of these two time note combinations: ♩. ♪ is the more common. This is how you count it:—

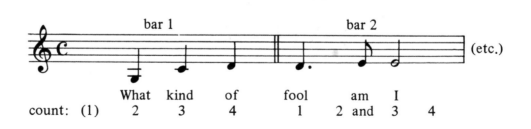

WHAT KIND OF FOOL AM I, p.30

Notice how the "dot" delays note D, so that the next note (E) falls on an "and" beat. The situation is always the same with this rhythm.

Look out for other examples of dotted quarter note/quaver combinations in the songs which follow.

WHAT KIND OF FOOL AM I

(FROM THE MUSICAL PRODUCTION "STOP THE
WORLD I WANT TO GET OFF")

Words & Music by Leslie Bricusse & Anthony Newley

Suggested registration: *piano*

Rhythm: bossa nova
Tempo: medium (♩ = 100)
Synchro-start, if available

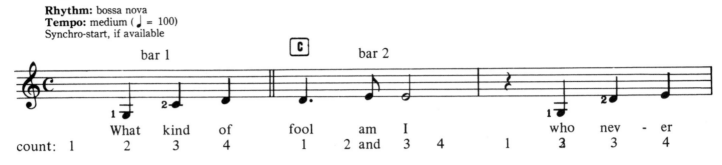

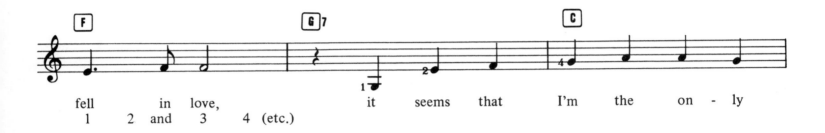

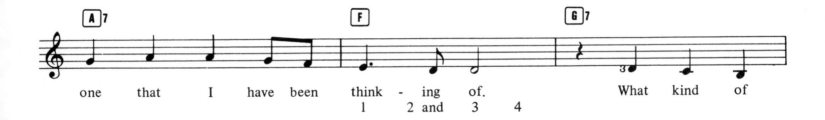

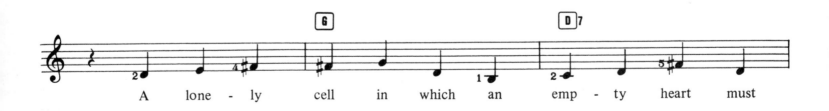

LOVE'S ROUNDABOUT
(LA RONDE DE L'AMOUR)

French Words by Louis Ducreux
English Words by Harold Purcell
Music by Oscar Straus

Suggested registration: accordion
+ arpeggio (if available)

Rhythm: waltz
Tempo: fairly fast (♩ = 160)

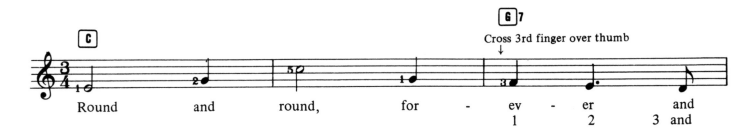

Cross 3rd finger over thumb

Round and round, for- ev- er and
1 2 3 and

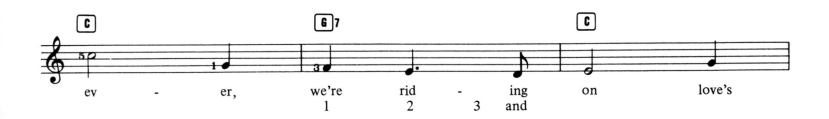

ev- er, we're rid- ing on love's
1 2 3 and

round- a- bout; rich or

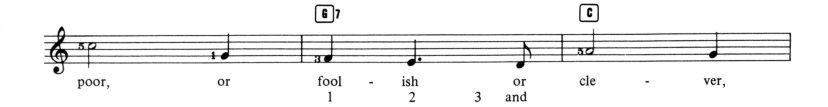

poor, or fool- ish or cle- ver,
1 2 3 and

round we must go, year in, year
1 2 3 and

STARDUST

Words by Mitchell Parish
Music by Hoagy Carmichael

Suggested registration: vibraphone, or celeste,
+ full sustain

Rhythm: swing
Tempo: fairly slow (♩ = 80)
Synchro-start, if available

CHORD OF D MINOR (Dm), AND CHORD OF A MINOR (Am)

Using single-finger chord method:

Locate D (the higher one), and A, in the accompaniment section of your keyboard. Convert these notes into "Dm" and

"Am" respectively (see Book two, P. 28, and your owner's manual).

Using fingered chord method:

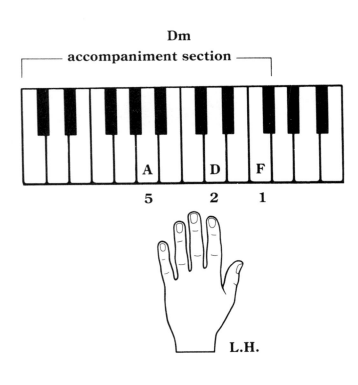

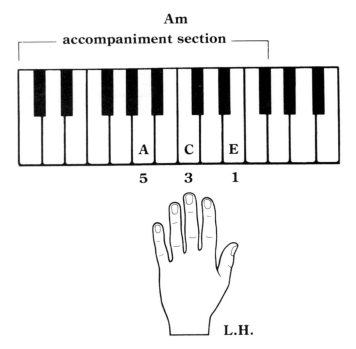

SCARBOROUGH FAIR

Traditional

Suggested registration: flute

Rhythm: waltz
Tempo: slow (♩ = 84)

New hand position

Cross 2nd finger
over thumb

Are you go - ing to Scar - bor - ough fair? Pars - ley, sage, rose - mar - y and thyme_____ Re - mem - ber me to one who lives there. She once was a true love of mine.

TAKE ME HOME, COUNTRY ROADS

Words & Music by Bill Danoff, Taffy Nivert &
John Denver

Suggested registration: piano, or electric piano
+ half sustain

Rhythm: swing
Tempo: quite fast (♩ = 192)

Al - most hea - ven, West Vir -

gin - ia, Blue Ridge Moun - tains,

Shen - an - do - ah Riv - er.

Life is old there, old - er than the

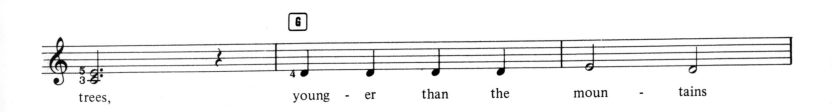

trees, young - er than the moun - tains

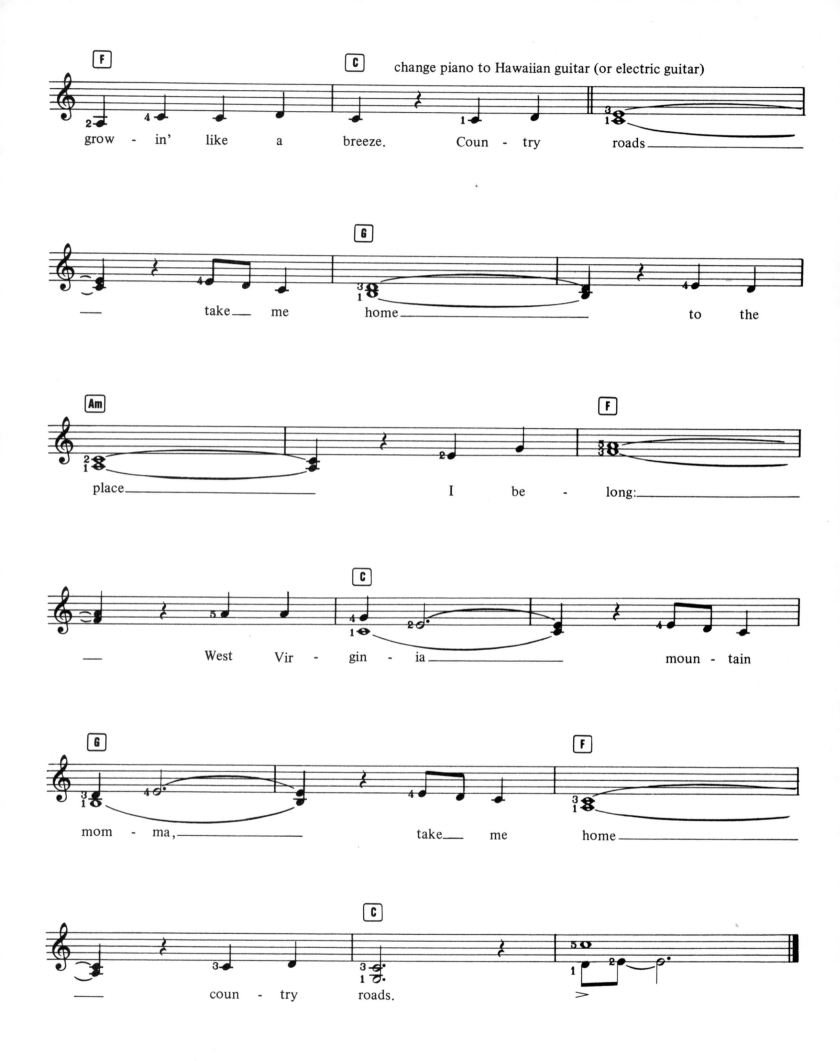

change piano to Hawaiian guitar (or electric guitar)

grow - in' like a breeze. Coun - try roads ____

____ take ___ me home _____ to the

place _____ I be - long: _____

____ West Vir - gin - ia _____ moun - tain

mom - ma, _____ take ___ me home _____

____ coun - try roads.

THREE NEW NOTES FOR RIGHT HAND:
HIGH A, B, C

If you have a 44, or a 49 note keyboard, these will be your top three notes.

I have placed letter names beside the new notes in the next few songs.

SAILING

Words & Music by Gavin Sutherland

Suggested registration: *jazz organ*
+ sustain

Rhythm: disco
Tempo: slow (♩ = 69); but run rhythm at double speed
(♩ = 138)
Synchro-start, if available

* Pause on each note, for dramatic effect.

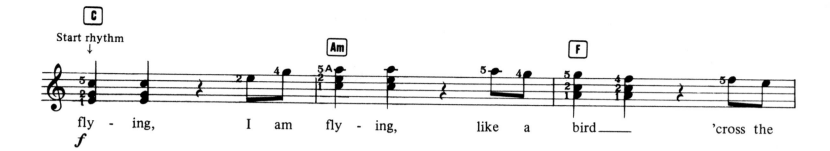

fly - ing,   I   am   fly - ing,   like   a   bird＿＿   'cross the

f

sea.   I   am   fly - ing,   pass - ing   high   clouds,   to   be

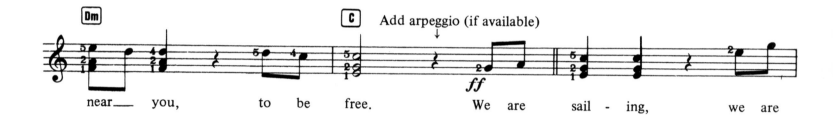

near＿   you,   to   be   free.   We   are   sail - ing,   we   are

ff

Add arpeggio (if available)

sail - ing,   home   a - gain＿＿   'cross   the   sea.   We   are

sail＿ ing   storm - y   wa - ters,   to   be   near＿   you,   to   be

free.   To   be   near＿   you,   to   be   free.

Stop rhythm

I CAN'T GIVE YOU ANYTHING BUT LOVE

Words by Dorothy Fields
Music by Jimmy McHugh

Suggested registration: piano

Rhythm: swing
Tempo: medium (♩ = 120)

I can't give you an - y - thing but

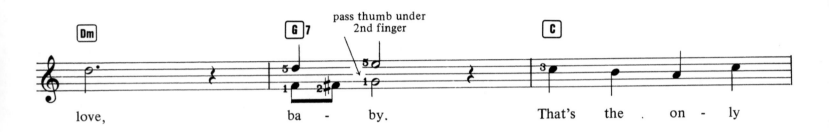

love, ba - by. That's the on - ly

thing I've plen - ty of, ba - by.

Dream a - while, scheme a - while, we're sure to

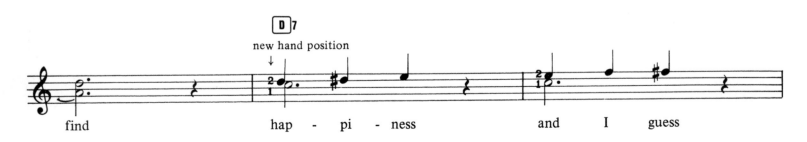

find hap - pi - ness and I guess

all those things you've al - ways pined for. Gee, I'd like to

see you look - ing swell, ba - by.

Dia - mond brace - lets Wool - worth does - n't sell,

ba - by. Till that luck - y day you know darned

well, ba - by. I can't give you

an - y - thing but love. *f*

CRUISING DOWN THE RIVER

Words & Music by Eily Beadell & Nell Tollerton

Suggested registration: accordion

Rhythm: waltz
Tempo: fairly fast (♩ = 152)

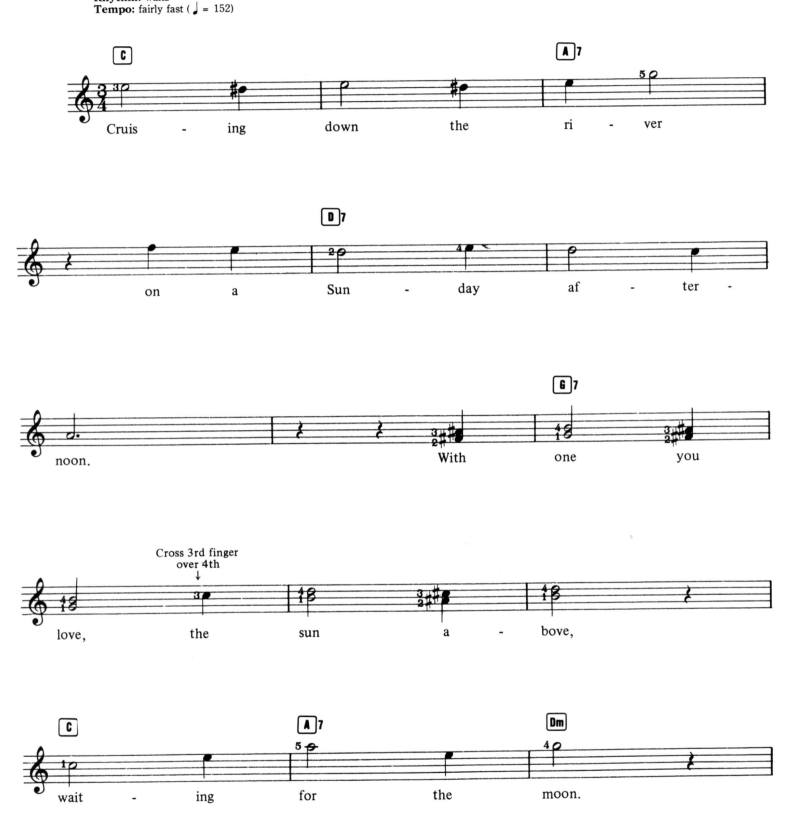

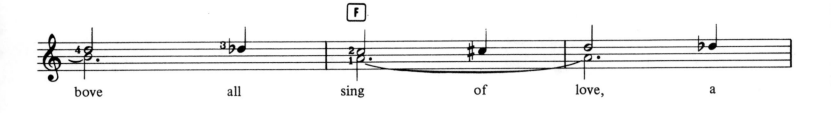

bove all sing of love, a

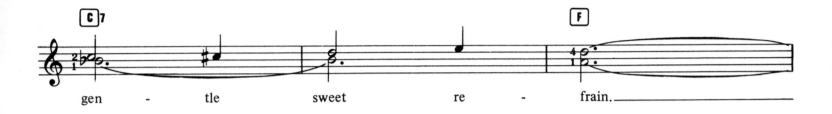

gen - tle sweet re - frain.

New hand position

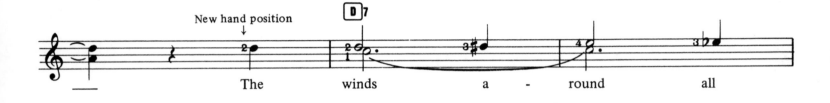

The winds a - round all

Squeeze together

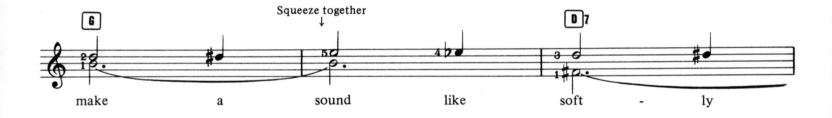

make a sound like soft - ly

flute to accordion   *D.S. al CODA*

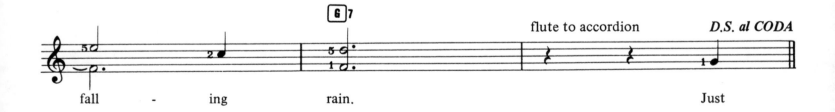

fall - ing rain.   Just

✦ *CODA*

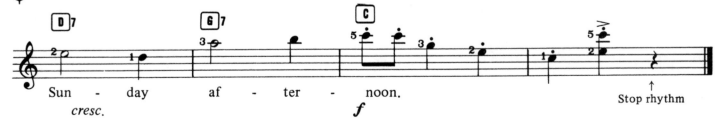

Sun - day af - ter - noon.

cresc.   *f*

Stop rhythm

HELLO GOODBYE

Words & Music by John Lennon & Paul McCartney

Suggested registration: electric guitar
Rhythm: rock
Tempo: medium (♩ = 112)

LAST WORD

Congratulations on reaching the end of Book Two of The Complete Keyboard Player.

In Book Three you will

- improve your note reading

- learn new chords

- play in new keys, including "minor" keys

- develop further your sense of rhythm

- add those important professional touches to your playing.

CHORD CHART (Showing all "fingered chords" used in the course so far)

C
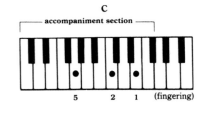

C7
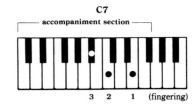

G
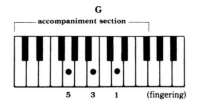

G7
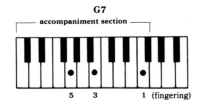

F
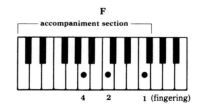

Fm
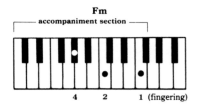

Dm
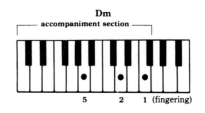

D7
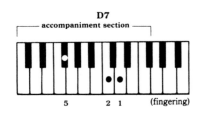

Am
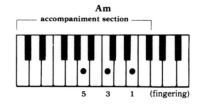

A7
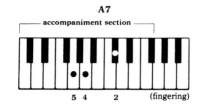

For all portable keyboards *by Kenneth Baker.*

THE COMPLETE KEYBOARD PLAYER

OMNIBUS EDITION

BOOK 3

Amsco Publications
New York/London/Sydney/Cologne

ABOUT THIS BOOK

In Book Three of The Complete
Keyboard Player you learn about scales
and keys. When you play in different
keys you make basic changes of sound,
and so add a new dimension to your
playing. Minor keys, especially, can
change the whole flavor of your music.
In Book Three you play in five new keys,
including two minor keys.

In Book Three you continue your left
hand studies, with the emphasis as usual
on "fingered" chords. Nine new chords
are introduced, in easy stages, and all the
chords used in the series appear in the
Chord Chart at the back of the book.

There is plenty for your right hand in
Book Three. There are double notes,
chords, fill-ins, counter-melodies, and so
on, and several new and effective tricks
of the trade, such as ornamental "grace
notes".

As usual, throughout the book you will
get tips on how to use the facilities of the
keyboard — the sounds, the rhythms, and
so on — more effectively.

Although Book Three continues in the
"teach yourself" tradition of the earlier
books, all teachers of the instrument will
want to make it one of their standard
text books.

CHORD OF E7

1 Using single-finger chord method:

Locate "E" (the higher one of two) in the accompaniment section of your keyboard. Convert this note into "E7" (see Book One, p. 42ff., and your owner's manual).

Using fingered chord method:

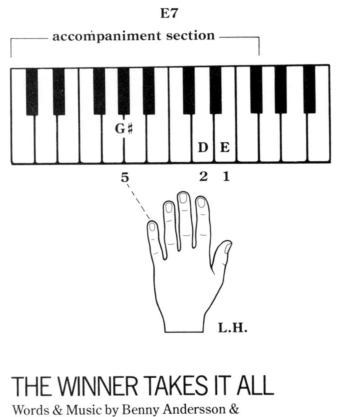

THE WINNER TAKES IT ALL
Words & Music by Benny Andersson &
Bjorn Ulvaeus

Suggested registration: piano

Rhythm: rock
Tempo: medium (♩ = 104)
Synchro-start, if available

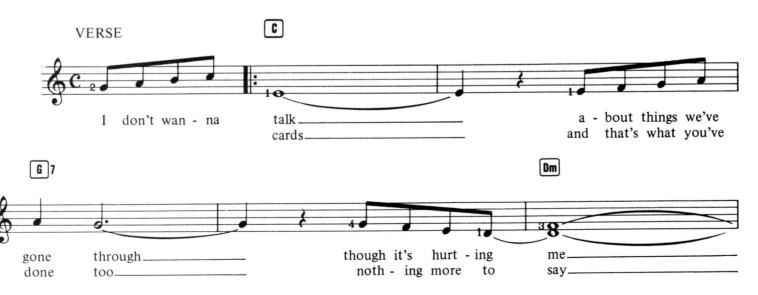

VERSE

I don't wan - na   talk_____   a - bout things we've
             cards_____   and   that's what you've

gone   through_____   though it's hurt - ing   me_____
done   too_____   noth - ing more   to   say_____

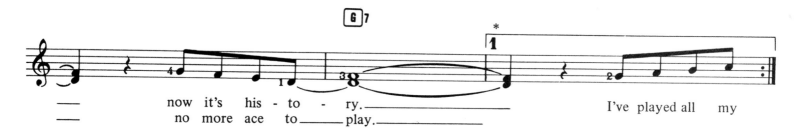

now it's his - to - ry._____ I've played all my
no more ace to_____ play._____

* 1st Time Bar. Play this bar on the first time through only (then repeat as marked).

CHORUS

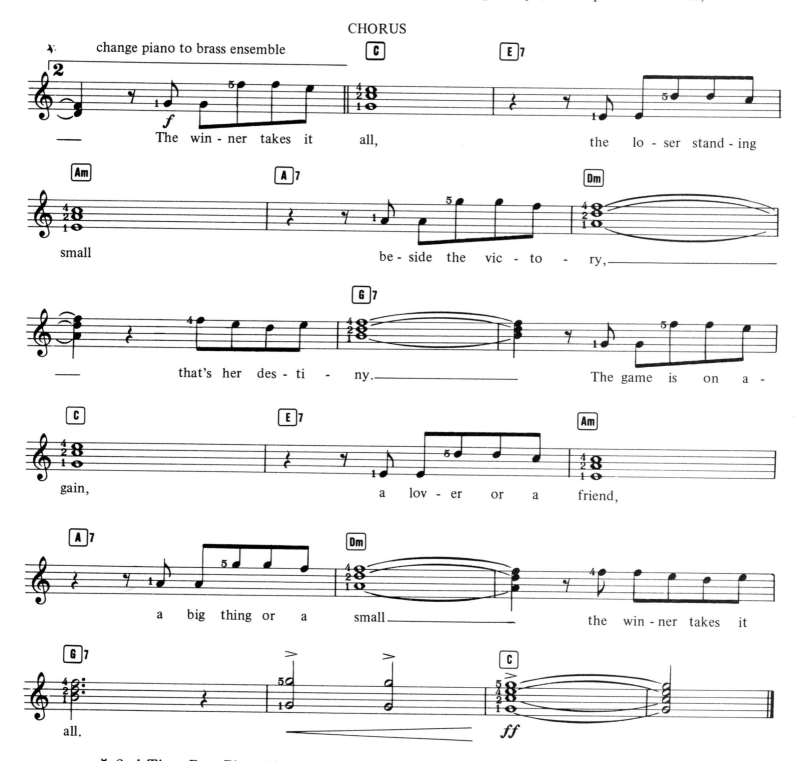

change piano to brass ensemble

_____ The win - ner takes it all, the lo - ser stand - ing

small be - side the vic - to - ry,_____

_____ that's her des - ti - ny._____ The game is on a -

gain, a lov - er or a friend,

a big thing or a small_____ the win - ner takes it

all.

* 2nd Time Bar. Play this bar on the second time through only (then carry on to the end).

I LEFT MY HEART IN SAN FRANCISCO

Words by Douglas Cross
Music by George Cory

Suggested registration: string ensemble

Rhythm: swing
Tempo: fairly slow (♩ = 88)
Synchro-start, if available

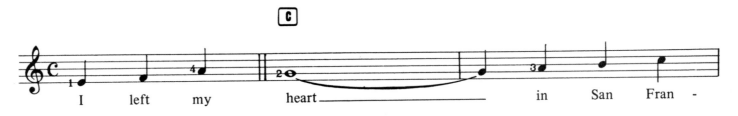

I left my heart _____ in San Fran -

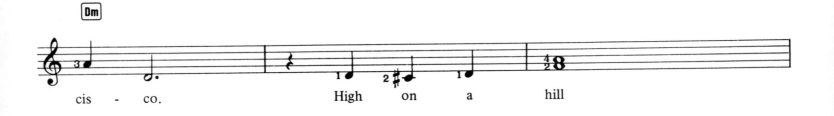

cis - co. High on a hill

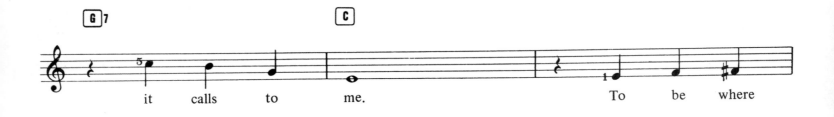

it calls to me. To be where

lit - tle ca - ble cars _____ climb half - way to the stars.

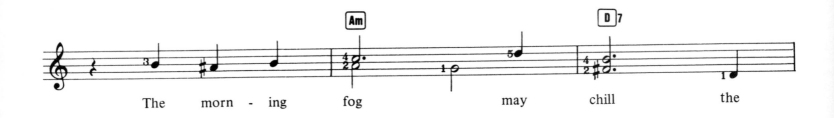

The morn - ing fog may chill the

CHORD OF E MINOR (Em)

2 Using single-finger chord method:

Locate E (the higher one of two) in the accompaniment section of your keyboard. Convert this note into "Em" (see Book Two, p.28, and your owner's manual).

Using fingered chord method:

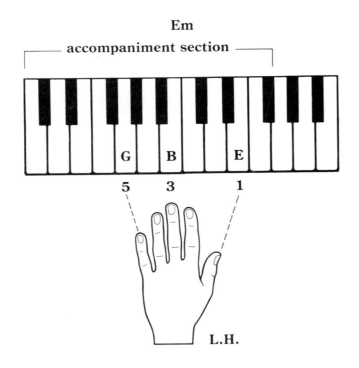

Em

CAN'T BUY ME LOVE

Words & Music by John Lennon & Paul McCartney

Suggested registration: synth-guitar + chorus (chorale)

Rhythm: rock
Tempo: fairly fast (♩ = 160)
Synchro-start, if available

VERSE
N.C.

I'll buy you a dia - mond ring, my friend, if it
Say you don't need no dia - mond ring, and___

makes you feel all right, I'll get you an - y -
I'll be sat - is - fied. Tell me you want those

thing, my friend, if it makes you feel all right.)
kind of things that___ mon - ey just can't buy.)
For

I don't care too much for mon - ey, for mon - ey can't buy me

CHORUS
chorus to tremolo

to Coda ⊕

love. Can't buy me love.___
mf

Ev - 'ry -bod - y tells me so. Can't buy me love.___

D.S. al Coda

tremolo to Chorus

⊕ CODA

No, no, no, no!
f

love,___ Can't buy me

love!___
f

↑
stop rhythm

THE SONG FROM "MOULIN ROUGE"

(WHERE IS YOUR HEART?)

Words by William Engvick
Music by Georges Auric

Suggested registration: hawaiian
guitar

Rhythm: waltz
Tempo: slow (♩ = 80)
Synchro-start, if available

When - ev - er we kiss, I

wor - ry and won - der, your lips may be

here, but___ where is your heart? It's

al - ways like this, I wor - ry and

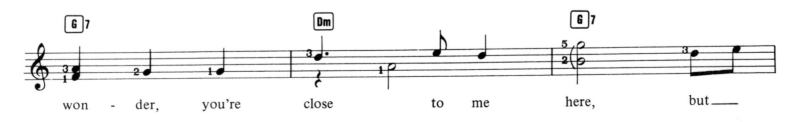

won - der, you're close to me here, but___

*split these two notes (playing lower note first).

10

where is your heart? It's a sad thing to re - al -

ise that you've a heart that nev - er melts. _____ When we

kiss do you close your eyes, pre - tend - ing that I'm some - one

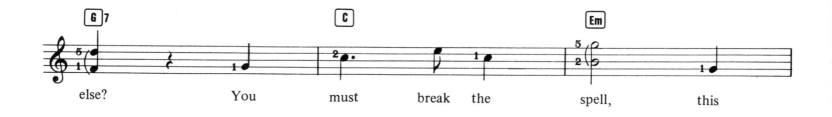

else? You must break the spell, this

cloud that I'm un - der, so please won't you

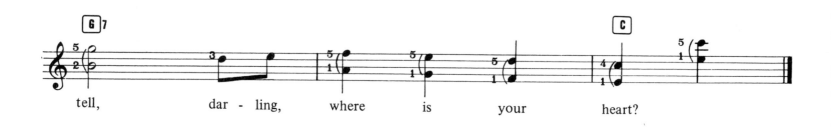

tell, dar - ling, where is your heart?

SCALE OF C; KEY OF C

3

A scale is a succession of adjoining notes:

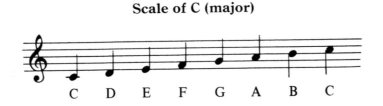

Scale of C (major)

C D E F G A B C

As you see, there are no black notes in the scale of C.

When a piece is built on this scale it is said to be in the "key of C". Almost all the pieces you have played so far have been in the key of C. The occasional black notes you encountered in those pieces were of a temporary nature only, and did not affect the overall key.

From now on you are going to play in a number of different keys for the sake of contrast.

SCALE OF F; KEY OF F

4

Scale of F (major)

F G A (B♭) C D E F

As you see, a B Flat is required to form the scale of F. When you are playing in this key, therefore, you must remember to play all your B's, wherever they might fall on the keyboard, as B Flats.
To remind you, a B Flat is inserted at the beginning of every line:—

key signature

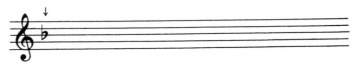

To help you further, I have arrowed the first few B Flats in the following songs.

CHORD OF B♭; CHORD OF F7

5

You need these two chords in order to play in the Key of F.

Using single-finger chord method:

Locate "B♭" in the accompaniment section of your keyboard. Play this note on its own and you will have a chord of

B♭ (major).

Locate "F" (the lower one of two) in the accompaniment section of your keyboard. Convert this into "F7" (see Book One, p. 42ff., and your owner's manual).

Using fingered chord method:

B♭

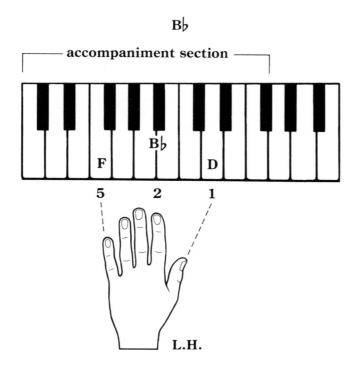

F7

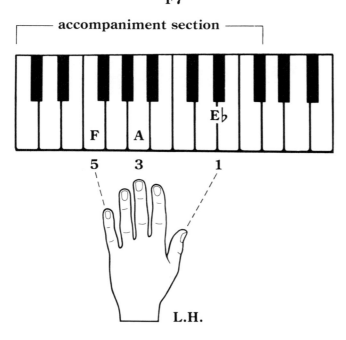

OB-LA-DI, OB-LA-DA

Words & Music by John Lennon & Paul McCartney

Suggested registration: funny

Rhythm: swing
Tempo: fast (♩ = 112)

* Cut Common Time. A feeling of two in
a bar (**2/2**) rather than four (**4/4**). Notice the
metronome marking: ♩ = 112.

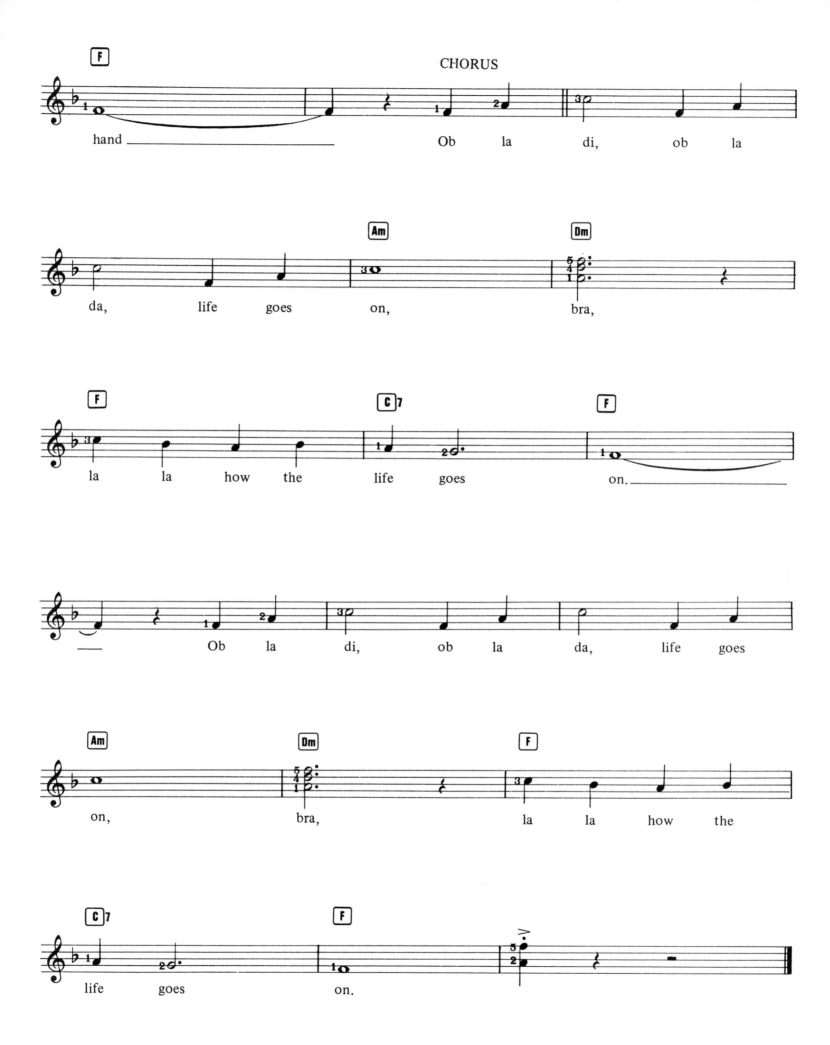

WHO CAN I TURN TO
(WHEN NOBODY NEEDS ME)
FROM THE MUSICAL PRODUCTION
"THE ROAR OF THE GREASEPAINT –
THE SMELL OF THE CROWD"
**Words & Music by Leslie Bricusse
& Anthony Newley.**

Suggested registration: string ensemble

Rhythm: bossa nova
Tempo: fairly slow (♩ = 92)

Who can I turn to,_____ when

no - bod - y needs me?_____ My heart wants to know, and

so I must go where des - ti - ny leads me._____ With

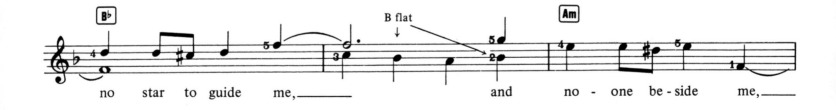

no star to guide me,_____ and no - one be - side me,_____

_____ I'll go on my way, and af - ter the day the

darkness will hide me._____ And may-be to-mor-row_____

_____ I'll find what I'm af - ter._____ I'll

throw off my sor - row, beg, steal, or bor-row my share of laugh - ter._____

_____ With you I could learn to,_____ with
cresc.

you on a new day,_____ but who can I turn to if
f

you turn a - way?_____ stop rhythm
ff

TULIPS FROM AMSTERDAM

English Words by Gene Martyn
Original Words by Neumann and Bader
Music by Ralf Arnie

Suggested registration: accordion

Rhythm: waltz
Tempo: fast (♩ = 184)
Synchro-start, if available

When it's spring a - gain, I'll

bring a - gain Tu - lips from

Am - ster - dam. With a

heart that's true I'll give to you

Tu - lips from Am - ster - dam. I can't

18

SIXTEENTH NOTES (SEMIQUAVERS), AND DOTTED RHYTHMS

6 An eighth note (quaver) can be subdivided into two sixteenth notes (semiquavers):-

eighth note   sixteenth notes

A dotted eighth note is equal to half as much again (see "dotted time notes", Book Two, p. 29), that is, three sixteenth notes:-

dotted eighth note   sixteenth notes

In practice a dotted eighth note usually pairs up with a sixteenth note:-

dotted eighth note   sixteenth note

Together, these two time notes are equivalent to 4 sixteenth notes, or 1 quarter note (crotchet):-

3 sixteenth notes + 1 sixteenth note = quarter note

The general effect of a passage like:-

is of eighth notes (quavers) with a "lilt".

The phrase "humpty dumpty" is a useful guide to this rhythm:-

say: Hump-ty Dump-ty Hump-ty Dump-ty

stress   stress   stress   stress

These uneven types of rhythms are often called Dotted Rhythms.
Look out for dotted rhythms in the next four pieces.

SCALE OF G; KEY OF G

7

Scale of G (major)

G   A   B   C   D   E   (F♯)   G

An F Sharp is required to form the scale of G. When a piece is built on this scale it is said to be in the "key of G". When you are playing in this key you must remember to play all F's, wherever they might fall on the keyboard, as F Sharps. The key signature, which appears at the beginning of every line, will remind you:-

key of G

key signature
↓

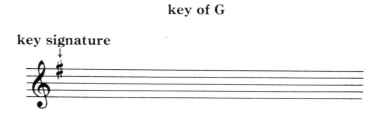

YELLOW SUBMARINE

Words & Music by John Lennon & Paul McCartney

Suggested registration: piano

Rhythm: swing
Tempo: medium (♩ = 100)
Synchro-start, if available

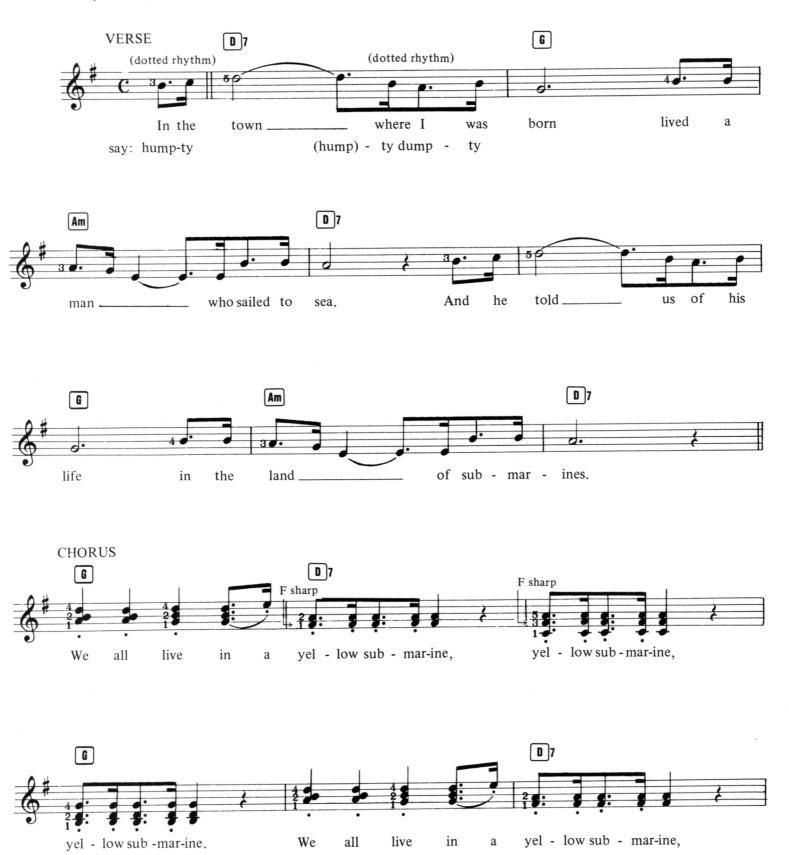

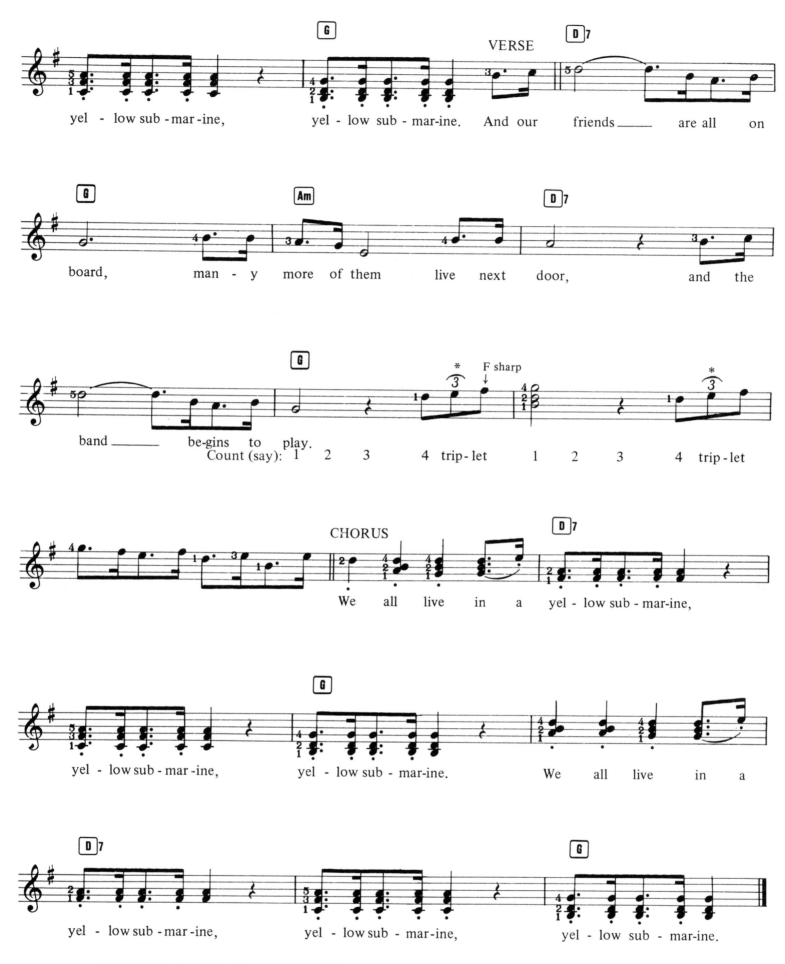

*Triplet. A triplet is a group of 3 notes played in the time of 2. These three eighth notes (quavers) must be played slightly faster than normal eighth notes, in order to fit them into the bar.

CHORD OF B7

8

Using single-finger chord method:

Locate "B" in the accompaniment section of your keyboard. Convert this into "B7" (see Book One, p. 42ff., and your owner's manual).

Using fingered chord method:

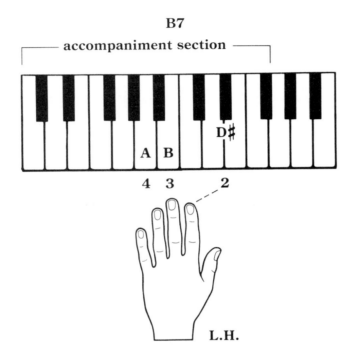

B7

CHANSON D'AMOUR
Words & Music by Wayne Shanklin

Suggested registration: clarinet

Rhythm: swing
Tempo: medium (♩ = 100)

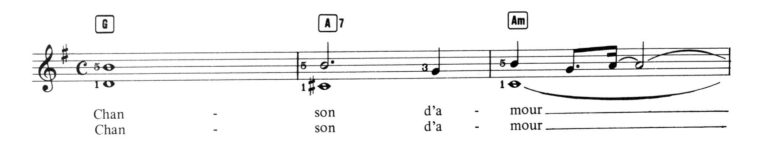

Chan	-	son	d'a	-	mour_____	
Chan	-	son	d'a	-	mour _____	

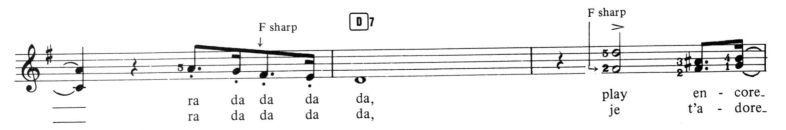

ra	da	da	da	da,	play	en - core
ra	da	da	da	da,	je	t'a - dore.

24

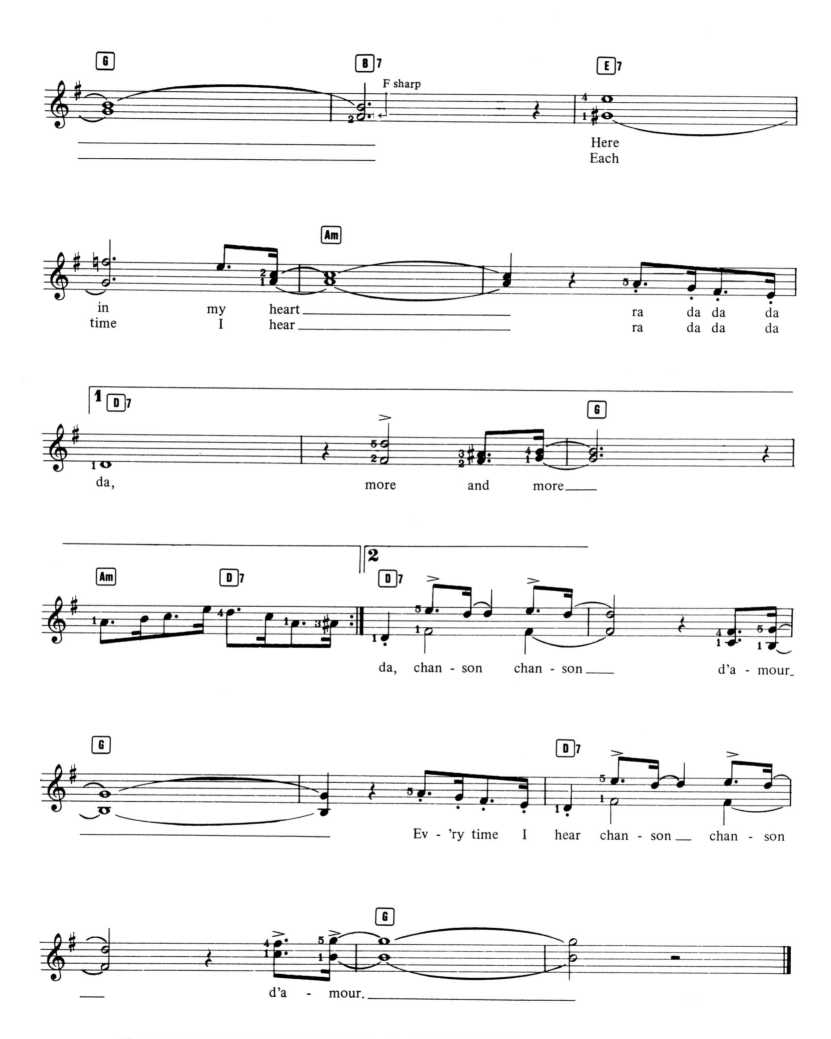

WHEN I'M SIXTY-FOUR

Words & Music by John Lennon & Paul McCartney

Suggested registration: funny +
duet (if available)

Rhythm: swing
Tempo: medium (♩ = 108)
Synchro-start, if available

When I get old - er, los - ing my hair__ man - y__ years from

now, will you still be send - ing me a Val - en - tine__

birth - day greet - ings, bot - tle of wine?__ If I'd been out__ till

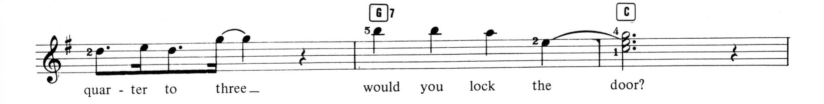

quar - ter to three__ would you lock the door?

Will you still need__ me, will you still feed__ me, when I'm six - ty__

Change funny to flute
FINE

four?

Ev - 'ry sum - mer we can rent a cot - tage in the Isle of

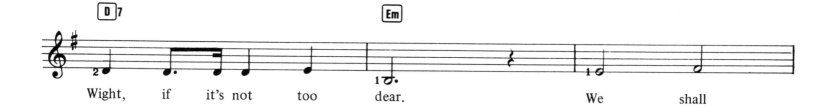

Wight, if it's not too dear. We shall

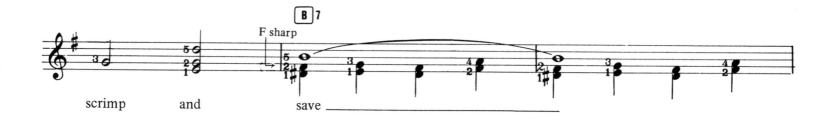

scrimp and save

F sharp

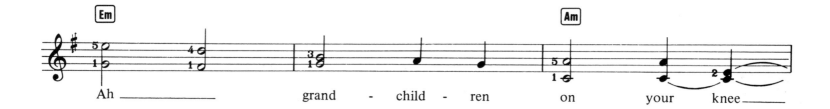

Ah _____ grand - child - ren on your knee _____

Ve - ra, Chuck, and

(N.C.)   ↓ flute to funny

D.C. al FINE

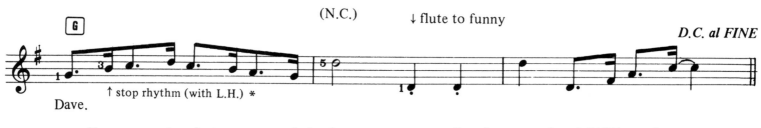

Dave.   ↑ stop rhythm (with L.H.) *

*leave synchro button on, and rhythm will start again automatically when you strike the next chord ("G", at the beginning of the piece).

CHORDS OF G MINOR (Gm), AND B♭ MINOR (B♭m)

Using single-finger chord method:

Locate "G" and "B♭" in the accompaniment section of your keyboard. Convert these notes into "Gm" and "B♭m"

respectively (see Book Two, p. 28, and your owner's manual).

Using fingered chord method:

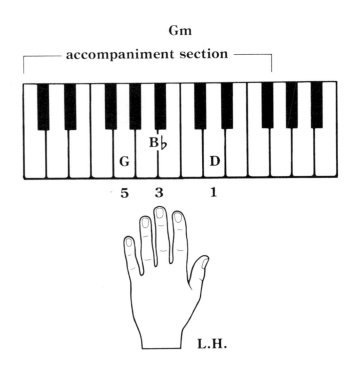

Compare this chord to G (major), a chord you already know.

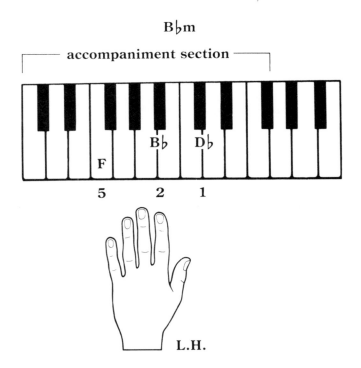

Compare this chord to Bb (major), a chord you already know.

THE WONDER OF YOU

Words & Music by Baker Knight

Suggested registration: electric guitar
Rhythm: swing
Tempo: fairly slow (♩ = 80)

*Quarter Note Triplet. 3 quarter notes played in the time of 2. Play these quarter notes slightly faster than usual in order to fit them into the bar, but keep them even and equal to each other.

THEME FROM POLOVETZIAN DANCES

Borodin

Suggested registration: flute

Rhythm: bossa nova
Tempo: medium (♩ = 92)

to Coda ⊕

change flute to clarinet

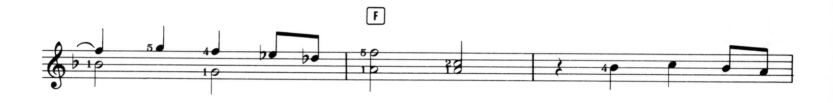

clarinet to flute
D.C. al Coda

CODA

MINOR KEYS

10 So far almost all your playing has been in major keys: C, F, and G. Songs written in minor keys, with their preponderance of minor chords, often have a sad, nostalgic quality, which makes an excellent contrast.

KEY OF D MINOR

11 The key of D Minor is related to the key of F Major. The scales on which these keys are built use the same notes:

scale of D Minor

D E F G A (B♭) C D

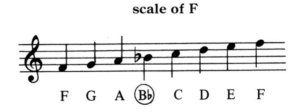

scale of F

F G A (B♭) C D E F

All the notes are white except one: B Flat. As you would expect, both keys have the same key signature:

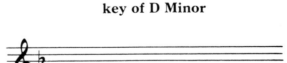

key of D Minor

key of F

When playing in the key of D Minor (as in the key of F), you must remember to play all B's, wherever they might fall on the keyboard, as B Flats.

LOVE IS BLUE
(L'AMOUR EST BLUE)

English lyrics by Bryan Blackburn
Original French lyrics by Pierre Cour
Music by Andre Popp

Suggested registration: harpsichord
Rhythm: bossa nova
Tempo: medium ($\quad = 88$)

HAVA NAGILA

Traditional

Suggested registration: clarinet

Rhythm: march $\frac{2}{4}$ (or swing)

Tempo: medium (♩ = 88)

* Grace Notes. Purely ornamental notes not included in the basic timing of the bar. Play your grace notes as quickly as possible.

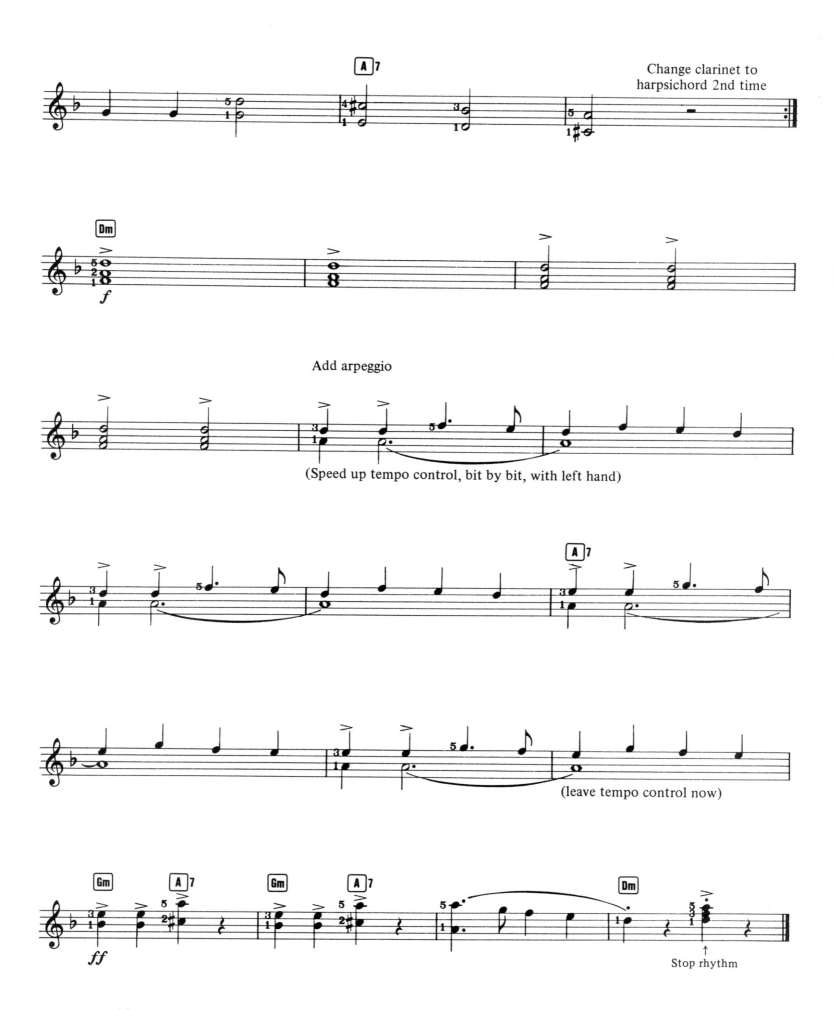

Change clarinet to
harpsichord 2nd time

Add arpeggio

(Speed up tempo control, bit by bit, with left hand)

(leave tempo control now)

Stop rhythm

KEY OF E MINOR

12 The key of E Minor is related to the key of G Major. Both keys use the same scale notes:

scale of E Minor

E (F♯) G A B C D E

scale of G

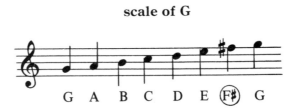

G A B C D E (F♯) G

All the notes are white except one: F Sharp.

The key signature is the same for both keys:

key of E Minor

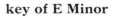

key of G

When playing in the key of E Minor (as in the key of G), you must remember to play all F's, wherever they might fall on the keyboard, as F Sharps.

THOSE WERE THE DAYS

Words & Music by Gene Raskin

Suggested registration: organ + tremolo +
arpeggio, if available
Rhythm: march , or swing
Tempo: bright (♩ = 108)
Synchro-start, if available

Those were the days, my friend, we thought they'd ne - ver end,
mf
la la la la la la la la la la
(start rhythm)

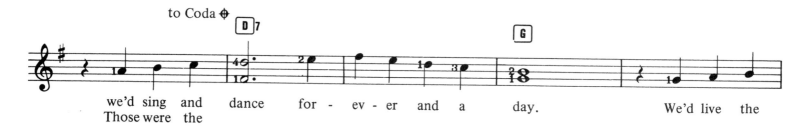

to Coda ⊕

we'd sing and dance for - ev - er and a day. We'd live the
Those were the

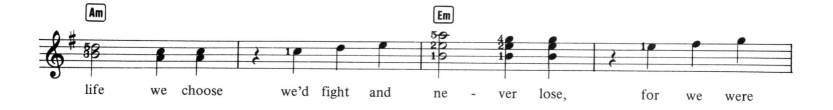

life we choose we'd fight and ne - ver lose, for we were

D.S. al Coda

young, and sure to have our way. la la la
f

⊕ CODA

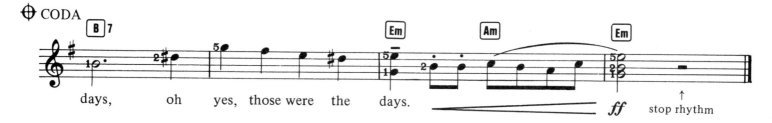

days, oh yes, those were the days.
ff stop rhythm

ANNIVERSARY SONG

Words & Music by Al Jolson & Saul Chaplin

Suggested registration: violin

Rhythm: waltz
Tempo: quite fast (♩ = 160)

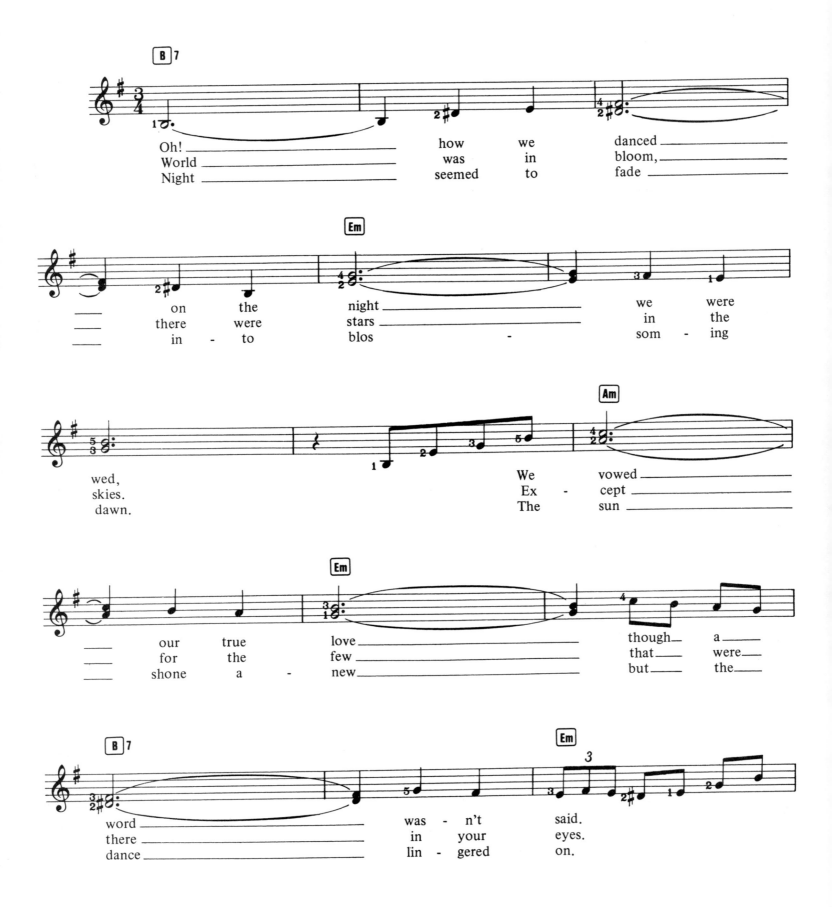

The

Dear, as I

held you so close in my arms.

An - gels were sing - ing a hymn to your

charms. Two hearts gent - ly beat - ing were

mur - mur - ing low: "My dar - ling I

D.C. al Fine
accordion to violin

love you so!" The

KEY OF B FLAT

13 The scale of B Flats, and therefore the key of B Flat, requires two flats: B Flat, and E Flat:—

When you are playing in this key you must remember to play all B's and E's, wherever they might fall on the keyboard, as B Flats and E Flats, respectively.

CHORD OF E♭ (MAJOR)

14 Using single-finger chord method:

Play the note "E♭" (the higher one of two) in the accompaniment section of your keyboard.

Using fingered chord method:

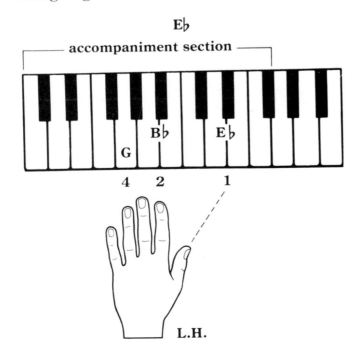

DON'T CRY FOR ME ARGENTINA

Music by Andrew Lloyd Webber
Lyrics by Tim Rice

Suggested registration: Trumpet

Rhythm: tango
Tempo: medium (♩ = 112)

MAMMA MIA

Words & Music by Benny Andersson, Stig Anderson &
Bjorn Ulvaeus

Suggested registration: synth. guitar

Rhythm: rock
Tempo: medium (♩ = 126)

VERSE

I've been cheat-ed by you____ since I don't know when.
So I made up my mind____ it must come to an end.

Look at me now____ will I ev - er learn?

I don't know how____ but I sud-den-ly lose____ con-trol

There's a fire ____ with - in my soul _____ just a

look and I can hear a bell ring ____ One more look and I for-get ev - 'ry-thing__

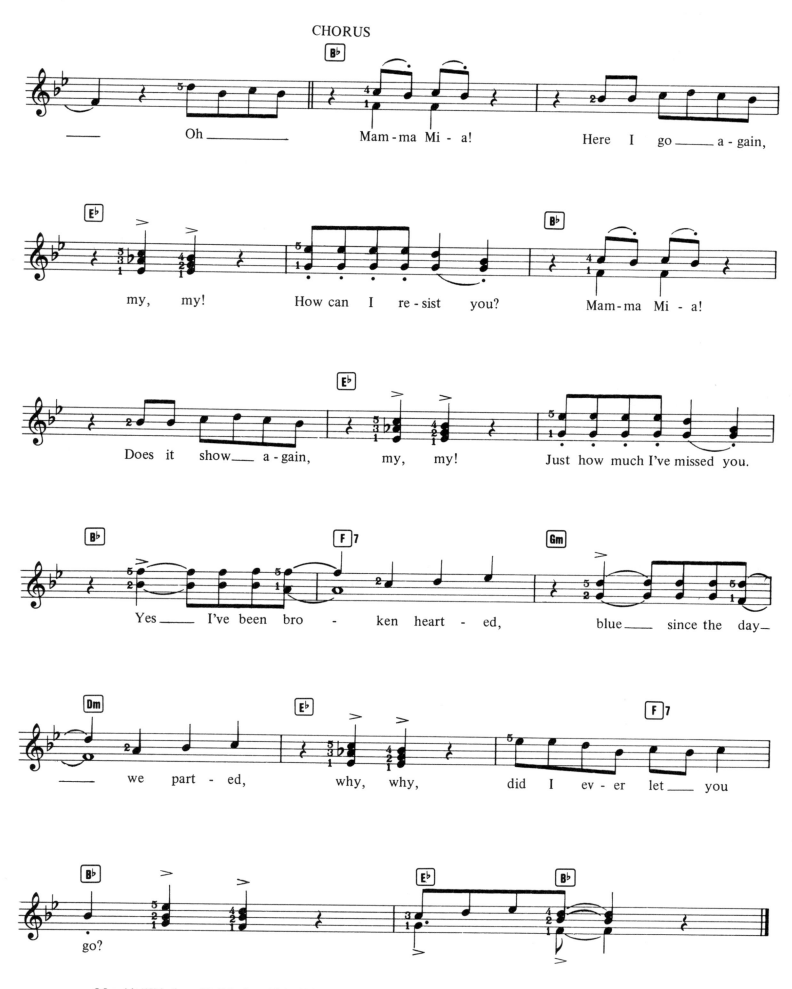

CHORD OF C MINOR (Cm)

15 Using single-finger chord method:

Locate "C" (the higher one of two) in the accompaniment section of your keyboard. Convert this note into "Cm" (see Book Two, p. 28, and your owner's manual).

Using fingered chord method:

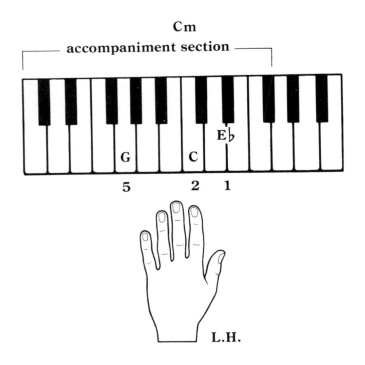

Compare this chord to C (major), a chord you already know.

RAINDROPS KEEP FALLING ON MY HEAD

Words by Hal David
Music by Burt Bacharach

Suggested registration: electric guitar

Rhythm: Swing
Tempo: medium (♩ = 104)

Rain - drops   keep fall - in' on   my   head,
did   me   some talk - in' to   the   sun.

TELSTAR

By Joe Meek

Suggested registration: jazz organ,
    with tremolo

Rhythm: disco
Tempo: medium (♩ = 120)

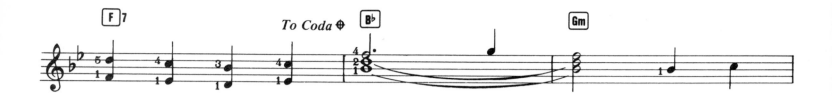

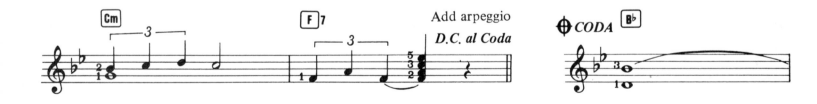

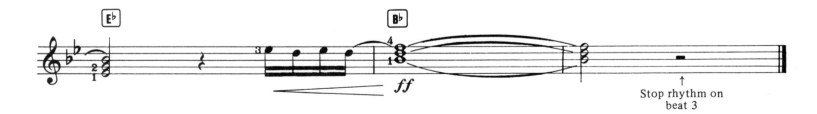

CHORD CHART (Showing all "fingered chords" used in the course)

C
accompaniment section
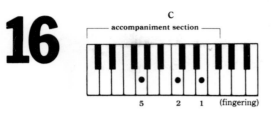
5   2   1   (fingering)

Cm
accompaniment section
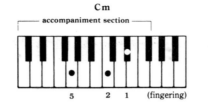
5   2   1   (fingering)

C7
accompaniment section
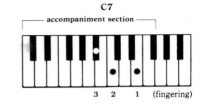
3   2   1   (fingering)

Dm
accompaniment section
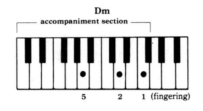
5   2   1   (fingering)

D7
accompaniment section
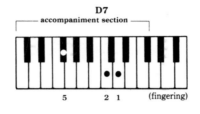
5   2 1   (fingering)

E♭
accompaniment section
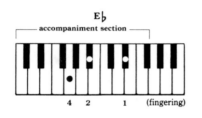
4   2   1   (fingering)

Em
accompaniment section
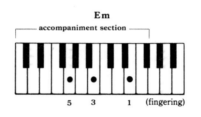
5   3   1   (fingering)

E7
accompaniment section
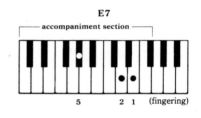
5   2 1   (fingering)

F
accompaniment section
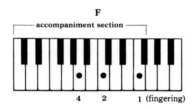
4   2   1 (fingering)

Fm
accompaniment section
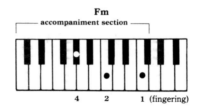
4   2   1 (fingering)

F7
accompaniment section
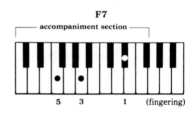
5   3   1   (fingering)

G
accompaniment section
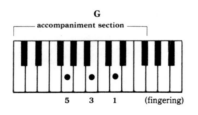
5   3   1   (fingering)

Gm
accompaniment section
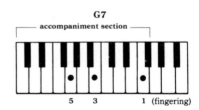
5   3   1   (fingering)

G7
accompaniment section
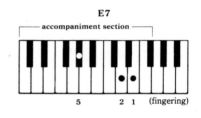
5   3   1 (fingering)

Am
accompaniment section
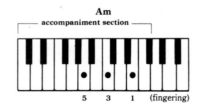
5   3   1   (fingering)

A7
accompaniment section
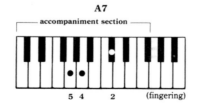
5 4   2   (fingering)

B♭
accompaniment section
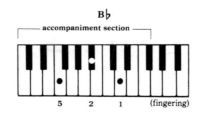
5   2   1   (fingering)

B♭m
accompaniment section
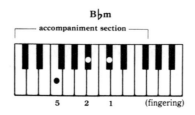
5   2   1   (fingering)

B7
accompaniment section
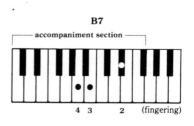
4 3   2   (fingering)